fresh ink

A COLLECTION *of* VOICES *from*
AOTEAROA NEW ZEALAND 2019

CLOUD
INK

First published 2019
Published by Cloud Ink Press Ltd, Auckland
P O Box 8988, Symonds Street, Auckland, 1150
www.cloudink.co.nz

ISBN 978-0-473-48928-1

Book Design and typesetting: CVD Limited, Auckland — cvdgraphics.nz
Cover design: Suzanne Day — suzanneday.nz
Printed by Ligare Ltd, Glenfield, Auckland — ligare.co.nz

Published with the help of

Kārearea, the endemic New Zealand falcon featured on the cover, is Aotearoa's most threatened bird of prey. To help ensure the voice of kārearea continues to be heard by future generations, a donation from the sale of each book will contribute to falcon conservation.

Contents

The Big Smoke

Vivienne Bailey

Eddie's toes wriggle, blocks of ice infiltrating his sleep. He wakes with a jerk, remnants of a dream swirling, messing with his head. Opening his eyes, he blinks against the muted sunshine. Slowly, he pulls himself upright. Hugging his bare arms, he runs hands over the clumps of erupting goosebumps.

The park is empty today apart from a bunch of teenagers hanging around the magnolia gardens. One of the youngsters has a skateboard under his arm. It looks like Will. Eddie and the boy had chummed up a few months back — Will sharing out squares of chocolate, Eddie oiling the skateboard's wheels. Eddie always keeps a bit of CRC handy, just in case.

Will reminds Eddie of his old mate, Frank. Gone now, but devilish, always up for a lark he'd been, just like the boy. He misses Frank.

It's cold today and balloons of dark cloud hang over the city. Eddie watches them cluster around the Sky Tower, circling the mast like a King Kong embrace. It looks like rain. He scoops up the worn, sand-coloured blanket. Once it had been bold and vibrant, as bright as a Queensland orange. Folding it tight, he shoves the bundle underneath the concrete step, close to his precious piles of cardboard. "Better than an armful of gold," Frank used to say about the collection of stiff board. And he'd been right, the material soaking up the damp, keeping it away from his sleeping body.

It hadn't always been cardboard and blankets. He and Frank had got work on Queens Wharf straight after they'd arrived. A bustling place, cargo ships, fishing boats coming and going, it'd been easy to get a job. They'd had lodgings in Fort Street, a roof over their head, beds to sleep in. But slowly the shipping world had changed, and huge steel ships replaced the smaller wooden vessels he and Frank had worked on. The talk had been all about exports, new fishing rules and regulations. They'd got laid off. It seemed no one wanted to take on a couple of aging "wharfies," no qualifications, bugger-all schooling.

"It's just temporary accommodation, Eddie," Frank had reassured him when they'd laid their cardboard and blankets under the concrete piles of the park's glasshouse. Eddie had believed him.

He straightens, unravelling the stiffness from his joints. Arthritis, the health nurse had told him. Too many nights sleeping rough, she'd rebuked. Yeah, Auckland's climate has filtered into his veins, alright. He stretches his arms, lifting eyes to the greyness overhead, and feels the first cold drops fall on his face.

* * *

Eddie's mum had stacked the branches of manuka inside the shed. He'd thought the slender twigs looked like baby trees, naked without their leaves.

"Get a move on, Eddie. It's gonna bucket down," she'd bellowed, her voice muffled, spiralling from the depths of the woodpile.

Eddie had run to the washing line, a piece of rope stretched between their house and the shed. The wind had whipped jeans, T-shirts, high above his head, twisting his sister's white school shirt tight, flicking fierce fingers through her navy blue skirt. The towels had smacked his face as he pulled at them, stinging his eyes. He'd been almost deaf to the throb of Frank's motorbike over the whistling sound of the gale.

"G'day, Eddie. How's it going?" Frank had silenced the noise, wheeling the bike under cover of the pine tree beside the house.

Eddie had squashed the washing against his chest and scarpered towards Frank and the house as the sky emptied the bucketloads his mum had forecast.

The three of them had sat at the kitchen table drinking mugs of sugared tea, waiting for the storm to pass. They'd listened to the wildness of nearby surf, pounding and smashing like a giant fist. Later, when the sun had come back, and the red-billed seagulls recommenced their whirling, Eddie had sat outside with Frank, sharing a joint. His mum had gone back to the woodshed. She hadn't approved of Frank and his motorbike.

"So, high school all finished. What're you going to do now, Eddie?" Frank had asked.

Frank was two years older than Eddie. He'd done seasonal shearing down on Blake's station. But he'd wanted to go up to Auckland, to find proper work.

Eddie had taken a deep drag on the joint, closing his eyes. He'd got pretty expert at this, thanks to Frank's tutelage.

Eddie's report had been abysmal: *Edward struggles with the complexities and constraints of learning. Reading is difficult for Edward and has held the boy back. However, he shows potential and with further application should succeed.* Eddie had been unsure what this meant. His mum had tried to help him read. She'd said he'd got dyslexia. It sounded like a foreign disease.

"Same as your Uncle Mike, it runs in the family," she'd told him, though she could read okay, filling in *The Dominion* crossword every morning.

"Dunno, there's no work on the coast. Guess I should look at getting something in town," he'd answered.

Town had been a small, dingy cluster of buildings, dulled by salt-lashed winds and burning sun. The tavern sometimes had work in the summer when the coast filled out with surfers and their Kombi vans. But that had been about all.

"Ever think about heading to Auckland, Eddie?" Frank had fired the question at him, squinting over the joint. "Have a go in the Big Smoke?"

"Um, maybe." Eddie had thought that idea sounded pretty scary, and he hadn't liked the thought of leaving his mum. Maybe Uncle Mike could come and stay, look after her and Janice, his sister? He could have Eddie's bedroom. Be better than that old caravan he lived in by the tavern.

The next week, Eddie had kissed his mum and sister goodbye. Clutching the brown paper bag of sandwiches, and a school sports bag stuffed with his clothes, not that there were many, he'd settled himself on the back of Frank's bike. Uncle Mike had arrived at the same time, together with Lucy, his big German Shepherd. The last thing Eddie had seen as they roared up the track had been his mum's face – her eyes shiny-bright, the hot sun triggering little rivers down her cheeks.

* * *

Eddie hears the town hall clock chime 4.00pm. He likes to sleep through the winter days; night-time he walks the pavements to keep warm. Summer is a different thing. He often wakes before sunrise, the mynas' raucous squawks puncturing his sleep. The city is balmy even at that hour, and it's easy to get going, a good time to find bargains, things other folk have left behind from the night. Sometimes, if he's lucky, he finds his special tipple, bourbon. It had been Frank's favourite as well.

He shrugs his arms into Frank's old leather jacket and starts towards the magnolia gardens. The bitumen path glimmers with moisture. Bending down, he reaches for a couple of cigarette butts, but his foot skids, slips against the slimy edges. His arm reaches out into nothingness. Tumbling, thoughts and body disarrayed, his head bumps and bangs across the shiny, black surface. Pain swirls through his arms, his legs. He tries to get up, but his whole being seems frozen downwards. Panic washes over him, reinforced by the persistent agony. Then a face appears, freckled, blue-eyed, peering down at him.

"Hey, Eddie," the face says. "You okay?"

Eddie's not sure. Blobs of crimson drip down from his head. They ooze over the path like leftovers from a vampire party. It freaks him out. Will stares at the blood and reaches for his back pocket.

"I'm ringing 111, Eddie. You look real bad."

They wait, neither of them speaking. Eddie is hurting too much to form thoughts, to utter words. Will is busy on his phone. The ambulance station is on the next block, and it doesn't take long for the green and yellow shape to pull into view. Eddie watches two blokes get out, carrying a stretcher and a long board. One lifts his head, shoulders and hips, while the other slowly slides the board underneath. Together they carry him and the mobile bed into the ambulance.

Will curls up in the seat beside Eddie, the skateboard between his legs. Just before the painkillers kick in Eddie opens his eyes. The pupils are wide and dark with the opioids.

"Look after my stuff, Will," he whispers. When the boy looks puzzled, Eddie tries again. "You know, boy, my stash of cardboard, my blanket." Will reaches towards Eddie, lays his hand over the older one. He nods and grins. Eddie closes his eyes, the corners crinkle a little. The boy's got an "it'll be alright" kind of grin. Just like Frank's.

__Vivienne Bailey__ is a Wellington-based writer and journalist with a public library background. Her work has appeared in the Dominion Post, NZ Lifestyle Block, Heritage NZ and Kiwi Gardener. In 2016, she completed Whitireia's New Zealand Diploma in Creative Writing. Her short stories have been shortlisted and placed in national competitions and also published in anthologies and online literary journals.

Fishing

Janet Pates

I knew an old woman who said she had a pond in her head into which things fell from her grasp. Names, faces, places all slipped away and were lost in the dark water.

Every day she fished in the pond with her memory stick and sometimes brought up fragments of her past: the smell of her mother's hair, the echo of a laugh, the colour of a dress she'd worn, aged ten.

One day, a young man came by. He had beautiful eyes. She knew those eyes. Was he, perhaps, her husband? But no, he said he was her grandson. So, she asked if he would take her home and he said, "Perhaps another day." Meanwhile, he would help her fish but what should he use for bait?

"Talk's cheap," she said. "But the written word is better." Then she handed him her memory stick and said, "Your turn."

Janet Pates *lives in the North Waikato township of Tuakau. Writing for children and adults, fiction and fact, she has been published in various journals and anthologies, including the School Journal. She is a past winner of the Tom Fitzgibbon Award for junior fiction and the National Flash Fiction Day NZ award*

Te Hau

Edna Heled

Today I need to inhale
more life volume
than yesterday

so I dress nicely
take myself places where I *think* I will find
the coffee blacker
the milk whiter
the cherries redder than donations of blood

I don't

so I go back home
undress
inhale my armpits

Te Hau (Te Reo Māori): air

Edna Heled *is an artist, art therapist, counsellor and travel journalist. She studied Art Therapy (MA) overseas and Psychology (Hons) in Auckland. Her writing includes short stories, poetry, and non-fiction.*

Lumi

Anna Knox

You couldn't understand why I wanted to come here.

It's the middle of winter, you said. No one goes north in winter. Let's go in summer when we can swim in the lake. I'm sure summer would be beautiful here. The lakefront cottages each a quiet world beyond the birch trees with their leaves like lace. The sounds of neighbours you never meet in the distance. Sauna smoke rising to the sky.

I want to see what it's like, I said. All that white. I've never seen it before.

In Helsinki, in the south, the snow falls clean and silent while we sleep but is old and grey by morning, crushed under cars and feet. I wanted to see snow that covered everything. I wanted to feel unearthly cold.

We arrived at afternoon, in the half dark, on a driveway carved through the snow. The scene was like a painting. Red farm buildings sat straight-edged around a yellow house glowing with lights. A dog ran up to greet us. Apart from the soft pad of his paws on snow there was no sound. I felt the dog's warm body through my gloves. He didn't pant but kept his mouth closed.

Conserving his heat, you said.

The farmer in his large black boots took us across the snow to the new sauna building, designed for conferences, where we would sleep.

Too cold for the lakefront cottages, you said. The ice gets in. In -25° you need bricks.

The farmer unlocked the door and handed us a key.

Dinner 17 o'clock, he said. His voice was deep and round. Come in house. Welcome.

Missä on sauna? I asked him.

He looked at me uncertainly. You looked at the floor.

It's better to speak English, you always say. The farmer removed his boots and we followed him through a large dining room and kitchen. In summer, the place would be full of families eating and drinking, or colleagues drunk and flirting. It was empty now. He opened a door and we surveyed the cold sauna. It was in the middle of the building, without any windows. We wouldn't be able to see the lake.

In the kitchen, the farmer pointed to a door which led outside. Huomio! he said, and mimed a banging motion with his hands.

Okay, kiitos, I said, although I had not understood.

You both smiled uncomfortably. The farmer said okay in a sing-song way, then left. I looked again at the door, not comprehending its finality and its danger.

After dinner we went to sauna. The fire was glowing red, perfect for löyly. I lay on the damp bench. You ladled water from the wooden bucket and threw it: one, two, three, four times. The hiss, then the puff, hiss and puff, and then – the wave of heat rolling in. Heaven. Hitting the head first, travelling downward over the body, then when it's over the skin like a shroud, seeping through to blood, muscle, bone, heart. Then returning, travelling back toward the face, where it burns a little coming out through your lips, like a spirit setting loose. Then the sweat finally, breaking out, and the body letting go, remembering a time before it was formed, returning to the air.

You went out to roll in the snow. I was mellow and warm. I said I would try tomorrow, took a beer, sat at the table to cool down. When you came back inside your eyes were lit up, your body covered with rough red patches, your face flecked with ice. When I gripped your arms and pressed my hips into your thighs your skin felt wet and dead.

Breakfast was served at the farm house. We crossed the snow in our fur-lined boots. Berries hung like drops of blood from twigs. The sky was bright blue and the ground ice white. Inside, the smell of cardamom and cinnamon filled the room: fresh korvapuusti sweating on plates. Slices of ruis-leipä, the dark brown dough like something deep in the earth, toppled over on the wooden board.

One of the farmer's children brought in coffee. The bitterness of green-roasted beans steamed from the pot.

Would you like some? she asked, in American TV vowels.

Yes, kiitos, I said. The coffee was hot inside my cheekbones.

After breakfast, we walked to the lake. The Highland cows were lapping at troughs of hot water. When they lifted their heads to look at us the water froze in quick icicles around their mouths. One came closer, curious, and put her head over the wire. I took a mitten off and stroked her thick, rust-coloured body.

The lake was a vast plain, the shoreline on the other side hours away. A metre out, frozen reeds stuck up through the ice.

What if it breaks? I asked.

It won't, you said. It's metres thick. I ran onto it whooping and jumping and sliding, but listening with my whole body for the fearsome crack.

Then, all at once, the dog came roaring out of the trees, past you, out onto the ice, and skidded over beside me. He put his paws up on my chest and pushed me down and I laughed. I felt ten years old.

On our way back, the dog went into a sudden, inexplicable frenzy and began digging in the snow. He got so excited that he barked.

Mad! I said.

No, you said. Look. There was a small, dark shape at the dog's nose.

A mouse, you said.

The dog nudged the little body, its tail frozen in an S. For a moment the dog seemed lost. Then he picked the mouse up in his teeth and trotted off.

After dinner, we went to sauna again.

This time, I said, I will roll in the snow.

It's easy, you said. Just a few seconds.

We went outside, steaming, without our towels, jamming the door open with a triangle of wood. You took my hand.

Go fast! you said. Or you will feel it! Ready?

I was not. Something felt wrong. I let go of your hand. I looked up. The stars were cold in the sky. You rolled down the slope with a whoop, then jumped up and ran back inside. The heat on my skin was thinning. I knelt down in the snow and laid my body out. It made a tinkling sound. It felt beautiful. I rolled down the slope and felt a rush through my body like stars. I shouted out for you, happy, and then I heard the door to the building close.

Did I hear it? I try to remember now.

I got up seconds later and going toward the glow I pulled the door, but there was a lock in it. A self-locking door and the triangle of wood was at my toes. **Huomio!** I pushed the handle down, up, down. The lock in the door remained. All in a shiver now, my feet freezingfrozen to the ground in a great ache. Bang bang bang on the door. But you were in the sauna, in the middle of the building exactly where a sauna shouldn't be, and no window. I banged harder, harder, harder. My skin started to prickle and burn. Then I was lost in the feeling in my hands. Then the door was a mattress on my fist and I wanted to lay down on it. I tried to lift my feet from the ground but they were struck. I had to pull and the skin peeled away on the ice, but I felt nothing. But maybe I imagined it.

My train of thought is losing itself.

You have not forgotten me. You are just not remembering me. You are thinking I am sitting inside with a beer. But you will remember. Out you will come, shouting, and take me in your warm arms and later we will laugh about this.

Soon, soon you will come.

I try the handle again but the lockers in the door but a little way along the wall are there windows I can break. The window will crack and sharp splitly and smear with blood. My fists are pillows. I punch the glass. It shumbles and rudders but it isn't breaken. I am cold and colder and colding and the quadruple-glazed glass wobbles like it's laughing. I need something harder than my pillowfists. I try my arm. My elbow. My head.

Glass denser than bricks.   Flocks and flocks of birds.

I am shaking like something possessed.

Then – a moment of clarity.

I can run to the yellow farmhouse! I can ring the bell and go inside to the warm, warm lights. I don't care that I'm naked. I run across the snow, exhilarant.

But under the snow are rocks, stones to mark a path, and I hit one with my shin and it cracks and I fell and here I am.

The snow has reached the hollows of my bones now. The only warm thing left is my tongue. I move it silently while I lie here, to keep the flicker in.

My heart is a blue stone. A pebble. A dead seed. My bones ache and burn.

I keep my mouth shut like the dog. My skin is frozen to the ice and will shred if I shift it. My lips are swollen out into the snow, or not there at all. I try to move them. Like a fish under ice, make an 'o'.

"Where are you?" I say, or I think I say. "Where are you?" I think.

My ears fill with white pain. It grows larger and larger, drifts out onto the snow. I will close my mouth to keep the heat in. Seal in my tongue.

Where are you?

Alone out here, slipping, I sense a little heart, like the one in the mouse, but come to life. A trickle of blood and then a rush and then a small thump and there it is: you won't notice that I'm gone. Not now, and afterward, after a few months, you won't notice that I'm gone.

You are still in the sauna, or drinking a beer. You are waiting for me but you are not concerned because that is not the way you think. You do not wonder what other people are doing. That is not the way you live. It is not neglect, but respect. It is almost love.

My body has gone now, is becoming snow now. If you picked up my arm it would melt in your hands. But I try to remember it as it was. Its heat. Its muscle and skin and bone. Its drama.

The thought of its old heat makes me cry and I think I feel something wet on my cheek.

The snow is melting me.

My thoughts of train are going.

I don't remember how time works but I think, perhaps, the window has passed.

The window? What will you see out the window?

A shape?

A shape on the horizon. I thought my eyes were closed but now I see a shape so maybe they are opening. Shall I tell you what I see?

I see the dog. Across the snow, which is white and growing whiter. He is leaping and bounding with his tongue hanging out. He is coming to me with his warmth. With his warm heart and his warm body and he will warm me up.

Anna Knox *is a graduate of the University of East Anglia (UEA) MA in Creative Writing (2010, Distinction). She writes reviews, essays, fiction and non-fiction. You can read some of her work over at The Spinoff.*

South Coast — Photograph by Crispin Anderlini

Old Man Edward's Box

Jacob Hagan

Old Man Edward told me never to go near the shed in the woods, but I came, whatever the rusted words he laid on me. This was my kind of living, doing what an old fool begs against, but in this case, I felt I had no choice. No choice to run the other way, no choice to let my instincts kick in. I felt especially magnetized to this violation, ever since I had come to visit the ashtray of my great-grandfather. This strange obligation came with the wind that wisped the farm for evermore.

Through my eyes was a motion blur of wood leaves and dirt. I was running away from the old man. It felt refreshing to leave that stuffy house of his; it felt refreshing to pump adrenaline through my blood. This was my release to the wild, to overcome the endless nagging of the wind.

What was inside that shed? Why would the wind challenge me to explore this shed 100 Edwards older than time? Why was Old Man Edward the lunatic he was? Would the answers come the faster I ran? I guessed so; I went faster than my legs assumed possible.

Inconvenience came as soon as I exhaled a breath of unawareness. A root, stretching like a sleeping cat, an identical blur to the leaves that blanketed the earth. The wind lets me feel many things – why not a feeling of avoidance, a single sign, of the devil of bike rides and forest runs? My body went flying for seconds; arms a windmill, my legs kicking like a looped animation, then pain whipped me like a slave. Dirt, pasting all my clothing but that wasn't near as attention-grabbing as my arm. It was in three pieces and it hurt like hell. It didn't stop me.

The wind was diminishing the pain. . .somehow. I climbed cautiously out of the ditch with my good arm, the only one left. I occasionally tested the broken arm with an outcropping root but it was defective. It was an uncomfortable feeling. I assumed it couldn't fix though, whether painful or not. If Edward ever saw me. . .

Crackkkkkk. . .

It came as soon as I stood up on the high ground. It sounded vaguely different from any old tree branch. I couldn't hear the thud of a fall. The source of the noise was right behind me. I felt its presence.

A door, synced its swings with the wind, the same wind that brushed me every step I took. I felt so close to the prize. When I slowly approached the door, a shape began to be differentiated in comparison to the undergrowth. A shed, choked by a factory of ivy. One of its walls, black, burned down and felled. Had Edward tried to burn this place down? The sudden rush of blood didn't stop me, no matter how hard I tried to run away screaming.

I questioned my life one final time, then entered.

It was a musty room, around three decades old, I guessed, ash particles adrift in the sunshine, spilling through the planks of the room. An eerie hum of silence vibrated within my bones. Was this the ghost of this abandoned monument or a figment of my imagination?

As I explored the forgotten mansion, a feeling came, a feeling of familiarity. I knew this place from the inside out but none had stood here even after I was born.

Tools rusted on their hooks along a long, dark block of wood. One of the items, a tool belt, would come in handy for my damaged arm. In all this rush, I had almost forgotten it was broken. It felt unnatural to pick the arm up from its limpness.

Almost a second later, an object animated from thin air and it woke in me an electric shock.

The ghost had arrived.

I turned to face it but there was no one there, until I looked down. A box – this wasn't here before – I was sure I swept every inch of floor with my eyes when I first entered. This was surreal. My head pulsed with untamed fear. Walls closed on me. I couldn't escape the grasp of the ghost of this cabinet.

It was taking control.

A foreign whisper rose from nowhere, speaking in a silent language. It was saying on a loop, "Open it and see what secret it hides." It felt soothing. It gave me courage. It made me unstoppable.

And so I reached for the nearest sharp tool, an axe. It seemed to magnetize on command but it was all the rush filling my head with superpower fantasies. My arm somehow healed after all. Then I hacked into the box, a strange approach with a box situation. Edward must've locked it and buried the keys, I assumed. It did no good to stop me and the ghost that had worn me like a shell.

I swung again and again with my two arms, the break now meaningless. Splinters flashed everywhere, stuffing my mouth and my eyes. I felt a million times stronger, stronger than the strongest man in history. Invincible.

Then in no time, the box barely resembled a shape. Not even a pile of splinters – the splinters were raked along the ground. But I wasn't interested in any shapes; there was nothing inside the box. I came all this way, broke my arm and all was futile. What was this thing? Whatever it was, I must've smashed its contents inside. The whispering had stopped.

I felt ashamed with myself. Angry . . . Sad . . . Lonely . . . Scared . . . Terrified . . .

I wanted to leave, fast. My control was shimmying back into play and so the rush of adrenaline came back bigger than ever. My thoughts were spiralling out and flurrying my head into fire until my voice let everything loose.

"What am I doing here? What am I doing here?"

My arm was throbbing again. . .and it was getting worse. The ghost had deserted me completely. I killed it I think. I could still hear its whispery voice though; it sounded like amused laughter. I couldn't run – the pain in my arm was too overwhelming – only lie in fear and pain as the ghost spat on me.

"I'm sorry, old Edward," I confessed. "I'm sorry I ever doubted you."

It turned to crying "Help," then it turned to the silence of giving up everything. The effort was futile – it only made my voice sore as well as my arm. Edward was nowhere near. No one was near. Not even the smallest forest critters. Only me, the shed and this ghost that would never die, no matter how many boxes I crushed. No matter the number of Edwards I disobeyed directly.

The process had begun.

The splinters left their resting on the ground and drifted towards me. I didn't care whether it was the breeze or something else entirely. They were piling around me like a castle then fusing together. It was a prison cell of splinters and it was metres high.

I tried to claw a hole out but the walls were already set. But there was still a hole to escape through – could I escape the ghost forever, using its abstract persuasions to lure me into this cage. I couldn't help it. I was ready to leap out before my time ran out, but my legs didn't obey. I couldn't escape. This wasn't happening. I needed to be free. I punched the wall with my only good arm but I was weakening, disconnecting from my body. The last of my senses available was my voice. I yelled while the opening was still large enough to hear through.

"Help me," I shouted with all my might. "Somebody help me!" It only took a few seconds till my voice cut off for good. Then my hearing. Then my eyes. I was unconscious and the box had pieced its final splinter into place.

* * *

The box is open and out I come, blinking at the sudden gush of light, take a small cough from the dust that floats by. This is only half of me, however; I am a shell accommodating a man called Harvey.

Harvey swings in joy – he hasn't felt this way in years. He's inhabiting a body he barely recognizes as his own but he never takes a glance of himself to acknowledge this. He is only grateful to be alive. Grateful for me. Grateful for every little thing that brought me closer to here. Harvey steps outside slowly – like the man who had first stepped on moon ground – and takes a long-lasting whiff of reality. He acknowledges nature at first, but he knows something much more important is at stake.

"It's time, Old Man Edward," he chants. "It's time to confront you like I did 30 years ago."

Harvey leaves his home and heads on a path towards his nemesis.

***Jacob Hagan** is a high school student in Whakatane. He enjoys writing and has a vivid imagination which he uses to create his stories. Jacob has had a short story published in the Young NZ writers 2018 anthology, 'Timegate to tomorrow' and has also achieved second place in the 2019 competition.*

Patience

Dave Moore

I give up waiting for the rain to ease, finish off my third pint, stand carefully and edge out through the narrow pair of pub doors. Gingerly. The heavy hinge springs try to push me off the crutches, and its slippery now as the rain has blown in onto the tiled steps.

It sweeps in heavier, stinging my face as I come out fully from under cover to cross the road, but I can't go faster to get out of it – I've learned that. I have to go slower the harder it rains, just take it, because twice I've been on my arse from trying to hurry. And then I can't sleep, from wondering what new damage I've done – what else have I fucked, will it need resetting? More days in hospital listening through the curtains to scared, bored patients and their exhausted women, who arrive with a smile then sit and worry: about the parking, about the bank, about him coming home so different. And being woken all through the night, please no. I've had enough of that.

I swing along carefully watching the ground ahead, not over-reaching and making sure the crutches find solidity. It saves me seeing my reflection in the shop windows – anyway; I know I look 20 years older. Two months since my right foot was on the floor, and another month to go. Head down. Concentrate. Then six months more at least to come, relearning how to walk – assuming I haven't done more damage on the way.

I'm starting to forget what it feels like to be standing upright. Even in my dreams at night I don't run or fight anymore. And being off work I talk to no one except the neighbour's cat, or the neighbour – about the cat; and I don't like either of them. So I had to get out tonight, get amongst normal people, but I should have believed the forecast. It feels such a long way home, like being a kid with short tired legs again.

"You're going not bad on those."

I look up from concentrating on the footpath and see a woman who'd been at the table next to mine earlier on in the pub. She's interesting and not too young and I would have attempted conversation, but she was sat with two couples.

She's leaning against the wet bench seat of the bus stop. It's the one outside the expensive kids' clothes shop that I've never seen anyone in. Her jacket has a fur-trim collar, but it isn't built for rain and I'm surprised she isn't obviously cold. The heels are like things my daughter always wanted to wear when she was with me. This woman could have been out clubbing, not hanging in the local on a weeknight. I stand straighter and take a rest on the sticks for a moment.

"Thank you. They don't like the wet though."

"No, of course."

I look towards the timetable on the post. "I don't think there's many this late. But I don't really know," I add unhelpfully. Fuck, I'm just so desperate to talk to anyone, I must sound like a half-wit.

"I know. I'm just waiting here – hoping the rain gets better before I walk." She smiles quickly then turns away, letting me know I can go. As she would – given that I'm clearly a desperate old pub dreg with no sense and less appeal. She has an accent I can't place, maybe Slavic but not quite. The face is pretty but also strong.

I think of telling her there'll be taxis but she'll need to phone for one down here – there's no cab rank – just to keep the talk going, but I don't. I move on, out of the shelter of the shop awnings and across the next street noticing again how steep the camber is up and down to the gutters – things I haven't been aware of since pram days.

At the top of the rise I stop and have a breather under the shelter of a thick low tree, which is keeping off the worst of the rain. I'm losing feeling in the little finger of one hand from the pressure. Must be trapping nerves or something despite having layers of foam wrapped on the handle of the crutches. They tell me I need the exercise, so I do it, but now I've got these other problems kicking in.

I rest the point of the moonboot's toe on the dark ground to take weight off my hip and back but the throb in the foot is too strong and I have to lift it again. I swing it like a pendulum front to back, then side to side. It feels better in some ways being up and moving, but I know it's doing harm in others; right up in my neck there's been a tension building in the last two weeks. The asymmetry gives me headaches and weird dreams.

The rain quietens off a touch and I see her heading up from the bus stop. She walks as quickly up the rise as she can on those heels. I wait and then move out to the kerb. She comes alongside as I wait to cross at the junction and glances down.

"How long are you in the boot?"

It's not that I go looking for it, but one consolation of having this thing is that at least you get chat and some sympathy. Like having a three-legged dog with you.

"Two months and one to go, non-weight-bearing."

"How did you do it?"

"I just got it wrong dismantling a scaffold tower at home, doing some painting. I came off, hurrying a bit when it started to rain. Bent the foot in half when I landed, and ruptured it long-ways."

We let cars pass, waiting for a big enough gap so that I won't have to rush.

"And how long do you think it will actually be before you are returned to function? How long are you prepared to be?"

Her tone takes me by surprise. I look sideways at her in the streetlights as we cross.

"It's going to take as long as it takes, I suppose. It's a bad one. They said it could have been worse, but not much."

"Of course it's bad. And you think this will help it Coming out drinking, when it's dark and wet when you can easily fall Overtiring yourself?"

I try to make light of it. I wasn't expecting to be told off. "Oh, you know – I was going crazy staying in. I just need to get out sometimes and. . ."

"And you think it is okay. Okay to not be patient. Okay to expect people to help you if you don't help yourself?"

She is walking at my slow pace but I want her to speed up. I want her now to leave me to inch slowly home. Instead, she steps ahead and turns, walking backwards to watch me move.

"That's not only three months. An injury like yours – that's a year, maybe two before you can do most things again. Maybe never."

"How do you know – about my foot?"

"Not just your foot – everyone's foot. I am nurse in Romania; we have the same feet. Everyone has the same feet. I do months in orthopaedic. Of course I know."

She steps back beside me and moves slowly, pulling her tiny collar up again as the rain swirls between big villas. I try to change the subject away from how long I have stretching ahead – before life becomes normal again or however close that will be to the old normal. I'm not ready yet to face a life too different.

"I thought you'd grab a taxi. Or get a lift home with your friends."

"I don't need the taxi; you need the taxi. This is just rain. And they are not really my friends."

"Are you a nurse now then? Where do you work?"

"I can't be a nurse here, only support worker. Same as those girls at the pub. I'm cleaning toilets and floors. These people, the nurses here, they want me to pay so much. So much, and to take exams I have already passed ten years ago, more than ten years. Who can afford that when they get paid almost nothing? I can't afford that."

The rain changes from hard to downpour and for a minute it hammers us, then stops almost instantly.

"I can't afford anything," she says. "I can't even afford a taxi after paying the stupid price in that pub."

Huge drops fall from the magnolia and moreton bay fig trees and the light wind under the aerial roots cools our skin and stirs the big soaked leaves above. I feel a trickle reach my instep, inside the sock, inside the jeans and inside the moonboot. The only warm part of me is the area on the foot where the nerves were cut in surgery.

She smiles, resigned. "I must be patient. But patient for just a year, like you – yes, that would be very nice. But no – I must be patient for a very long time, I think."

We walk on, her knowing the pace I need. I hesitate at the corner where I have to turn left off the main road. She flicks her head down the short avenue: "You go this way?" I don't want to ask which way she's going, in case it's a different one, which I'm sure it is.

"Yeah. I'm about three streets down. No, four."

She steps carefully around a big steel plate covering some work in the footpath and waits for me, silently critiquing my limitations.

"What is your job?"

I hesitate, which she notices. "I'm a construction manager."

"But . . .you're not sure?"

"No, I'm sure. I am."

"But. . ."

"But I'm not sure when I will be again."

We move carefully down the narrower, darker footpath and away from the main road, in the quiet tree-hung street. It feels warmer.

After a few houses have passed, I realise she has been waiting for me to think through what I just said, about my job. She didn't fill the space with another question, and I'm grateful for that. People have generally been trying to make me feel better by platitudes, telling me I'll be good as new soon, how everything will be back to normal before I know it. I realise I don't know her name.

"I'm sorry." I look up from the footpath, turn and find her eyes as we approach the only streetlight on this side. "I'm Nils, by the way."

She looks back from gazing into the lit windows of the houses and flats we're slowly passing. Thinking about the other lives going on in each one.

"Ana."

I think about stopping so I have a hand free to offer to shake but she waves me on. "How old are you?"

"Forty-seven."

"You have to climb ladders, and cranes and things like that, in your work?"

"Sometimes."

"Then you should be doing something else anyway. And your foot will never be as it was, I know – I have seen many. At some point you must know that, so know it now, Nils, and start to do other things."

I wait until she turns her face and raise my eyebrows. "You're very blunt."

She shrugs as she stops and puts a hand on my shoulder to take off her heels, then walks on in bare feet despite the cold wet.

"I'm 36. I live with my mother who tonight made me so mad that I dressed up like a teenage hooker so I would piss her off, and went out to waste money getting drunk with people who I do not like, and who do not like me."

I laugh. She doesn't. Just carries on, serious-faced.

"I was married, but I'm not now, and I'm very glad that it is over and that I am here instead. I have no children, but one day? Sooner not later, of course. I like men – not women – for sex, and when I can be a nurse again I will have goats."

I have to stop for a moment to rest the foot and look down to hide the smile. Ana looks away, shyly hiding her eyes for the first time.

"I'm sorry, you do not need to know all of that. And my mother is wonderful and has been through a great deal. But sometimes. . ."

I look up and can see in the dim light that she has her bottom lip between her teeth and may be close to crying. She lifts a foot to brush gravel from the sole and I move closer so she can place a hand on my arm. She thanks me.

"How do you say that, thanks, in Romanian?" I ask.

"Mulțumesc."

"Multimesc."

"Close."

"We move on, but slower now, saying nothing.

At my gate she hangs her shoes on the fence, asks for my phone and glances at the numbers at the head of my list before putting in her own number. I drop it back in my pocket and get ready on the crutches to move up the path.

"Thank you for walking me home."

"That's okay. It was too early to go home anyway – my mother would have said it was proof she was right – that no man in this place would want me."

"Well, pleased I could be of some service."

She looks at the house. Reading the stories told by the footwear by the door, the length of grass, the choice of colours of the new paint I was three-quarters through applying when I leaned back overloaded with tools onto a scaffold rail I'd already removed. She picks a head of lavender from the hedge, rubs and sniffs it.

"Mm. And also, when I get back, please text me in an hour. Say, 'Thanks for great evening, hope to see you again.' Just that, no jokes – or she will know."

"I can do that. Anything else?"

She smiles and puts the lavender in her jacket pocket.

"Maybe another in the morning when she is in the kitchen alone. Just before 6.30 when I am in the shower. She always looks at my texts then because the charger is by the jug. She thinks I don't know. Be keen, but a little nervous – get something wrong, so send another. Yes, send two."

"I will."

"Yes, you will."

She combs her fingers through her wet hair to help it dry, unhooks her shoes from the fence and tiptoes across the wet grass of the berm sensibly scanning for dogshit. At the curb she turns but it's dark and I can't read her face for clues as she calls. . .

"Noapte buna frumosale."

***Dave Moore** is a New Zealander born in London. He has lived in Auckland since 1990 and completed the AUT Master of Creative Writing in 2016. His work has appeared in Fresh Ink 2017, Landfall, and Year's Best Aotearoa New Zealand Science Fiction & Fantasy: Volume I (2018).*

Ko Kau Te Kete

Vaughan Rapatahana

Vaughan Rapatahana *is widely published across several genres in both his main languages, Te Reo Māori and English. He is also a poet, with several collections published – in Hong Kong, Macau, the Philippines, USA, England, France, India, and New Zealand. His Atonement was nominated for a National Book Award in the Philippines in 2016. He won the inaugural Proverse Poetry Prize the same year and was included in Best New Zealand Poems in 2017.*

'the kete is empty,'
were his own bereft words.

his head shook,
an oversized version
of one of these cheap bobbly toys
bought rashly from some two dollar shop
and stowed against the weary rear window
of a rusted jalopy.

his flailing eyes were an identikit of
the vertigo swirl on those murdered LPs
stowed déshabillé behind the tuneless piano,
while his tongue shot in and out/out and in
in slow-motion amphibian impersonation.

'poems, I can't do them anymore,'
he keened arrhythmic,
raising his arms
as if seeking absolution
for the missing muse,
the forsaken pages,
that *ramshackle* laptop
                                        dusty on the table,
burnt out & barren,

            w o r d l e s s.

as   o u t s i d e   on the scrawny lawn —
                                              the anorexic dogs whined
                                        for the kai
    he could   no   longer   provide.

[*ko kau te kete* – Māori – the kit is empty
kai – food]

Earth Warriors and Pale Frogs

Kayleen Hazlehurst

Hydrangeas cover the door to the greenhouse.
Frogs come up the toilet. You've seen them. Pale things.
"Put down the lid," you say, "it will keep them out."
I say, "I've not seen them."

I worry about bush fires.
You're surrounded by trees, cannot drive.
You say you can out-run a bush fire.
I say, "Don't be silly, 'course you can't."

A tsunami might hit the coast.
Exactly when, they're uncertain. Be prepared.
'Tidal waves', we used to call them.
Beset. Is this how our parents felt during the war?

You worry about dryness, the garden.
I keep an eye out for storms and floods.
Fish are drowning in a sea of plastic.
We're saddened. How can we help the fish?

I say people will learn to do better.
They will learn how to rescue the planet.
'Earth warriors', we used to call them.
You laugh and say, "So we did."

In the meantime. . .
Let's keep the toilet lid down.
Just in case pale frogs come to visit.
. . . "Cup of tea?"

__Kayleen Hazlehurst__ grew up on a farm beside the Mahurangi River and spent her teenage years involved in theatre arts in Auckland. Later, she studied anthropology and filmmaking in Canada and more recently has won recognition for her poems and short stories. Kayleen has nearly completed her second novel. Her genre is a lyrical blend of romantic historical fiction, war stories and family sagas.

The Price

Karen Phillips

In the end, there was no drama. Stephen quietly signaled Kevin and I to stay at the end of the Monday morning briefing. He handed each of us an envelope. I'd noticed them as we sat through yet another PowerPoint presentation promoting the great benefits of the almost-completed merger. The stark white envelopes were out of place on the polished plane of his otherwise empty desk – relics of more gentle times when decisions were written on paper and a company not so easily deleted as it is on a screen. Stephen was brought in from overseas to streamline data systems between head office and the branches and, somehow, he's ended up as our Auckland manager. Never met a bloke who can wrangle his way into as many talkfests as he does.

"Sorry guys," he said.

Kevin laughed. "No hard feelings. Already polished the golf clubs." He'd signalled earlier that he wanted no part of the after-merger structure, which he referred to as a corpse. He's 66 and wears his SuperGold card like a badge.

Stephen held out his hand to me. I shook it with difficulty.

"Sorry," he said again, then turned and walked out of the room.

Execution over. What kind of man can pretend to consider suggestions from a colleague whose warrant for execution lies on the desk in front of him? I felt like a fool.

We're an agricultural supply firm with branches throughout the country. I started in one of those branches and I still enjoy going back to visit. The storeroom smells of pig tucker and dog biscuits, but there's a camaraderie that's missing from the corporate office – the small-town friendships that extend beyond the supply yard stacked with shining rolls of fence wire and coils of black and yellow drain pipe. Our head office is in downtown Wellington, about as far from a farm as you can get and still live in New Zealand. It's a top-heavy setup with fairly big administration offices in both cities. Darned if I know what all these managers do all day other than have meetings and produce memos, which I've learned to ignore because a contradictory memo will be along in a few days. It's been a bit harder to ignore the company's failing financial position.

"It's early days," I told Denise when rumours of the proposed merger surfaced months ago.

"Maybe you should start looking for something else. Just in case. . ."

Denise frets about things, so I didn't tell her that I'd been looking at other options for the past couple of months. Not in any serious way, of course, but just generally keeping a bit of an eye open. It doesn't hurt to look. Actually, it does hurt to look. The view's pretty bleak. These days, companies want young guys with a trail of degrees after their names – not older men who sometimes make notes on paper. Wellington churns out pages of staff hiring guidelines to ensure that we do not discriminate against specified target groups – Māori and Pacific people, women, the disabled. Whoever writes this stuff should include older white men.

"There'll be lots of consultation before anything happens," I assured Denise. "The regional managers will be fine. They can't do everything from Sydney."

It turns out that they think they can. From the first whisper of change, the signs were everywhere that this merger would be different and yet I thought that if I kept my head down, I'd survive. I lied to myself and now I'm scared.

Redundant. That which can be omitted without any loss of significance. Me.

An empty office lies next to mine. Ray, whose office it was, read the signs and walked away six months ago. For a while the door remained open; there was talk of taking on a new central manager then, with a stroke of a Wellington pen, the regional boundaries were redrawn and the central region followed Ray into oblivion. His office became a storage room for cleaning supplies and boxes of toilet paper. Even then I refused to hear the message that the closed door shouted. I needed this job. There's not much in the bank and I'm not quite old enough for the pension. There've been restructures before but each time the axe has swung either high or low. It's always missed my neck. A few of the established systems get lopped off to be replaced by months of chaos then things settle and staff find their place in the new pecking order. The girls stop complaining about the colour of their latest uniforms and we stumble along, business as usual, but with a different logo and stationery. The one certain thing about a restructure is that everyone is expected to do more work for no extra pay.

According to the title on my payslip, I'm the accounts manager for the northern branches. The scope of my job description unofficially widens the more Stephen is out of the office doing what he calls networking and I call bullshitting his way to the top. In reality, I'm the go-to person for everything here in the Auckland office: from giving boyfriend advice to Kathy, the just-left-school receptionist, to training Braden, who's not much younger than our son and my assistant, although he's more interested in studying Kathy than agricultural accounts. When he's not studying Kathy, he's studying his phone. On our last visit to the branches, he could barely tell the difference between a bag of dog biscuits and a sack of wheat without first checking the brand names on his phone.

"You can smell the difference," I told him.

"Smell?" He looked puzzled as if I'd asked him to do a completely foreign action. "Why would I do that?"

Perhaps these young guys should do a stint in the regions to learn first-hand about the seasonal flow of operations and that the people who work there are more than numbers on a distant city database.

The news that I've been fired reaches my office before I do. Viv, my secretary, tells a caller that I'm tied up in a meeting for the next hour. Pete, one of the IT guys, leans out from his office further down the hall.

"That's bad news," he says, but the relief that it wasn't him this time shows on his face. He has a new baby and his wife doesn't work.

The envelope lies on my desk while the day takes over. Most of the smaller branches are being closed for good, larger branches downsized to agencies stocking shelves of glossy photos instead of the real product. I know these employees, understand their distress. When they ring, I want to help but I don't know what to say. I'm as deep in the same sticky mud as they are. At precisely 4.55pm, Viv's computer sings its shut-down song. She stacks her work in preparation for the next day, picks up the mail from the outer office (because the girls forget in their rush to leave the office on the dot of five) and checks to make sure that there's nothing more I need her to do – which I interpret as *I know what I'm meant to be doing.* Fifteen years of working together and by now I've learned who's the office boss and it's not me.

"Good night," I call to her as she walks out.

The hum of computers dies away. The bright green lights of the photocopiers fade to orange rest mode as the early evening quiet seeps through the empty offices. The hills behind the city are tucked tightly under a dark blanket of sleet. When I step out of my office to look along the corridor, I hear a murmur behind Stephen's door, then Kevin's voice rings out with laughter. Stephen's door opens, light spills across the carpet. Kevin walks out.

"See you Friday," Stephen calls after him.

Kevin's footsteps sink into the deep carpet of the corridor. I don't want to see Stephen right now so I turn back into my office to read the letter he gave me earlier. The letter is on the new orange and green stationery and signed by the boss from Sydney. In the early stages of the merger talks he attended a few staff meetings and came across as a decent sort of chap. He certainly had all the right jargon when he outlined the proposed shape of the new company that would arise from the ashes of our demise. He wanted us *to understand that the merger was a business decision in response to economic pressures, a partnership enabling us to achieve positive outcomes in this changing market.* The staff would be *consulted.* Job losses would be *contained* and *retraining offered where appropriate.* He thanked us all for *sharing this time* with him.

"What a load of crap," Kevin said. "He's their slash and burn man. I could smell the matches in his pocket."

"There's no logic in slash and burn," I argued. "It makes more sense to go slowly and work out where the changes really need to be made." I had a bit more to do with him when he flew over about three months ago to study the individual branch accounts, but I didn't know that he was in the office today.

I open the letter. There's a format to these things. I wrote a couple myself in the early days when I was a branch manager. It's a hard thing to do when you live in a small town and know you'll meet the recipient of your letter in the street or your kids are friends with their kids. It's especially hard when you know that there's little likelihood of the person finding another job, at least not locally. First is a paragraph of praise and thanks for loyal service, then an outline of the current circumstances. I skim through the first two paragraphs, head straight for the third. *Effective immediately.* The words leap out. I'm confused. This can't be right. I read them again. Effective immediately. Immediately? Today? This evening? I read further but the words are a jumble of nonsense sliding down the page. It can't be immediately. I have things to do tomorrow. When I look up, Stephen is standing in the doorway.

"What's this *effective immediately*?" I ask.

He shrugs. "It's what it says."

"What about Kevin?"

"He's gone."

"Without saying goodbye?"

"The Sydney office is putting on a farewell function on Friday evening. That's what I want to talk about."

My mind scrambles for something to anchor me to the foundation of life as I know it. "I can't go right now. Who's going to take care of the northern branches?"

Stephen's silent.

"Well, what about them?" I ask again.

His eyes slide around the room.

"I guess they're coming under my jurisdiction." He sees the look on my face. "Just for now," he adds quickly.

"What? You're taking over my job? How long have you known about this?"

He looks at me. "Look, I don't make the decisions," he blusters. "Your branches have a lot of slow payers and Sydney wants things done differently."

Over the years I've allowed the branches to accommodate the twists and turns of their customers' lives as best as they can and for the most part this has worked. "At least my branches don't lose clients," I say.

"Slow payers drain profits," he argues.

"They always pay in the end. Overall, my branch profits are as good as any other."

"They could be better."

He turns, leaves without saying anything more and I finally accept that in his eyes, I am a liability in the company ledger, a unit surplus to requirement, obsolete.

Stephen's young, aggressive and that's what seems to count these days. In Stephen's book, staff are company units to be used with maximum efficiency, shifted from here to there as required, dumped when past their *use by* date. Now tasks are allotted set times – so many minutes for unpacking product, a different number of minutes for stocking shelves. Stephen's produced a whole textbook, well, app, actually, of guidelines for client interaction. Profits in most branches are slightly up this year, for sure, but the grass growth during the exceptionally mild spring meant that lamb losses were low, milk production up and the farmers were happy. Happy farmers spend money. Once, when I asked Stephen to compare the effects of his changes with the impact of the brilliant spring weather, he muttered that the seasons were irrelevant because they couldn't be controlled. If your business relies on the seasons, shouldn't that be the most relevant factor of all? Braden and I toured our regional branches recently. I found bags of calf milk powder left to rot in the rain because the yard staff had no time to store them in the shed. In another yard, ten-litre containers of weed spray were piled, forgotten, in a corner. I'd wondered about internal theft when I looked at that branch's stocktake sheets. There was no love for the company anywhere and no biscuits for morning tea. Stephen might boast about improved efficiency and profit but he has no idea of what he's done. I came home feeling that I was on the losing side of a war.

I think back to when Denise and I got married. The car broke down on our honeymoon. Denise's brother towed us home. At lunchtime, we ate pies in a small, dusty park, the sun warm on our shoulders, the tow rope hanging slack between the two cars. We were pretty sure that our car was beyond repair but we weren't too worried – we'd sort something out when we got back so why not enjoy the sun and the pies? It's been a long time since we had a car like that, a long time since we were so unafraid. What is this fear, this anxiety that silently drips through the soul like a drop of rain that slides unnoticed through a tiny hole, then quietly builds up in the darkness of the roof space until one day it spreads a stain that can't be ignored across the ceiling? In the after-work quiet of my office, it hits me that I've paid a price for the nice house in a good suburb, the new cars, the overseas trips. I paid with the day that was no longer mine, the worries that kept me awake at night – the overloaded credit cards, the red figures shining at the bottom of the bank statement after the kitchen renovation undertaken to increase the value of the house, we told ourselves, but really because we saw something and wanted it. Instant gratification justified because *we work hard so we deserve it.* I kept on paying because that lifestyle grew around and through me until it was me. Who would I be without it? I allowed my life to hang on the barely recognised signature of a bloke 1,200 kilometres away and now the shining veneer has been shattered by the quiet fall of a sheet of paper.

Over the years, I've learned to listen, to analyse, then cut through problems as a plough blade cuts through the soil exposing the rich underside to the sun. I fold a sheet of paper in half and write *Problems* on the left and *Solutions* on the right. Usually, the physical movement of the hand across the paper helps the thought process in some way that I can't explain, but this time my mind stays blank and the pen rolls uselessly between my fingers. The problem is *redundancy.* I can't think of anything to write on the other side.

I screw up the paper, throw it in the bin, place the pen neatly back into the drawer. I remove the three family photos from the wall opposite my desk. When I leave, all that will remain of me is the brightness of the paint beneath them. That's a hard pill to swallow. I place the photos in my briefcase, close the office door behind me and walk down the empty corridor. For the last time, my footsteps echo around the vast marble cavern of the foyer. As I leave the building, the dark-tinted doors hiss quietly shut behind me.

A shower of rain has washed the car fumes from the air and the puddles on the road shine with the rainbows of water on oil. Shop windows throw coloured light across the footpath just as they did yesterday and all the days before that, just as they will in the days to come although I won't see them. There's something strangely comforting in that. A small crowd is gathered at the crossing opposite the car park, their faces as anxious, preoccupied, impatient as mine was yesterday when I also faced the slow commute home, the evening rush of dinner, a snatch of TV before diving into the paperwork that should have been completed earlier. I can't help but smile because tonight my normally heavy briefcase rests lightly in my hand.

I can't see the future but for the first time in a long time I know exactly where I am. The invisible axe finally fell. My neck is sore but not severed. I don't know what the cure is or how long it will take but there's something else.

Relief: the removal of anxiety.

I breathe deeply and the cool evening air fill my lungs. My shoulders relax and I walk towards my car.

Karen Phillips *began writing in 2009, winning the Katherine Mansfield Novice Writer Award that year. Since then, her short stories have been placed in competitions and published in takahē, Flash Frontier, and Fresh Ink. A Question of Blood, a collection of stories, was published by Steele Roberts in 2017.*

Ten-Minute Ciggie Break

Edith Poor

Ellen sat outside under the fluorescent light having her first ciggie in a year. It was a small garden in the place that they rented, concrete instead of grass and high walls of theirs and others closing it in a little square. Nearly all of it was taken up by the washing she'd done that day. Washing that fluttered in the breeze she didn't feel. Like little ghosts of the day before.

Next door they were having a party – or was it in the alleyway next door to next door? She couldn't tell – and while she sat in her bathrobe sucking on the stick in her fingers, she listened to them talk. One girl was talking more than the others. A boring, young American.

The girl was telling a story that no one was listening to. She couldn't stand girls like this, unattractive intellectual types who thought their stories were clever and people just didn't "get" them. Ellen wanted to scream at them when they asked her what she did all day and they responded with blank faces. Ellen wanted to spit at them and rip their breasts off with her teeth, but she'd vowed a long time ago to be more peaceful.

This girl was still talking. She'd hit the punchline of this story, which as far as Ellen could tell was as limp as the girl herself. The girl pealed off into laughter that no one else joined in. Ellen would have died if it were her. Ellen was good at telling stories, when she used to go to parties.

The silence lingered for a while and Ellen peered through the fence. It was incredible they could let her sit in that embarrassment for so long, but they'd just left and moved inside.

She remained cross-legged, looking through the fence to the neighbour's garden. A nice old couple – the guy was from a European country – Poland, she thought – and the woman hadn't ever spoken around her so she didn't know. But they both rode bicycles together in the weekend and Ellen liked them for it. It was sweet they still did stuff like that. Got out and about and all that.

She balanced her tea on top of her knee as she dragged again at the smoke. Didn't even like smoking anymore, but in moments like this it felt good – like she was in a movie or something, like someone was watching her and they'd call CUT soon. Didn't even really like drinking tea either but she'd tried to cut down on the booze in the last few weeks. Her daddy was a drinker and she hated her boyfriend asking her how much she'd had to drink.

He'd told her at dinner that night that when she stared in his eyes so much it was threatening. And she'd told him "I was just thinking that I love you." Which was a lie. What she was actually thinking was *I can't stand you.* He'd lectured her again on things he'd learnt that day and wanted to know why she'd even pretended to have an opinion on things she didn't even know about.

Did she realise she'd changed her argument four times and couldn't stick to a point? Or was it just that she wanted to be contrary?

Ellen hadn't realised, of course, and she said, "You're right" and "I'm sorry." And then they'd sat there in silence until they walked home and she took a shower and he bought cigarettes and then she'd pinched one and now voila! she was here. Hey presto. Like magic.

It was apparently autumn in Sydney but it was still warm and Ellen wondered if she could get away with not having to buy a jacket this time round, this time in winter. They'd moved here a year ago for his studies and she hadn't got used to the heat yet. She liked the flowers, though. The frangipanis that peeled themselves open for summer – she liked that – it was a trade-off for always feeling suffocated.

Before she'd sat here alone, she'd caught him having a cigarette out the back and asked him *What's wrong?* And all he'd said was he was thinking. Without turning back to face her. She saw his outline so clearly there in the fluorescent floodlights. An imposter in their garden.

"Baby?"

He spoke small at the door behind her. She didn't turn. Touché. She could be so calm when she wanted to be.

"You're smoking."

She'd stopped at this point, letting it burn out in her fingers, but for good measure she took a drag on it now before stubbing it out beneath her jandal.

"Yeah."

He moved to the chair in front of her and took her hand. He tried to catch her eye but she wouldn't look. At dinner she'd vowed she would never look at him again as long as she lived. A small protest.

"Why are you smoking?"

"Because I felt lonely."

"Oh."

He bowed his head to her hand and in the light, she could see how thin his hair was. Parting at the middle and at the back, revealing his pink scalp. It was greasy from the product he'd lathered through it and it hung in clumps, making the scalp more visible. It was soft and secret like the back of an ear and it made her stomach seize because she supposed they both were older now.

Brushing his lips against her fingers, he murmured "I'm sorry". And in this floodlight in their garden in Sydney she realised she would marry him. Because anything else was too hard. And she didn't know what to do.

***Edith** Poor is an actor and writer living and working in Auckland.*

Conversations in Therapy

Claire Hagan

1: Drinking Thinking

"So, you had a lapse.

What can you do today to make it not a relapse?"

I read and re-read those words you know. Over and over.

"You could come over today if you felt you needed to."

Each individual word. I scrutinised it. Searching for some hint of recrimination, disgust, frustration. Something.

My bag at my side in the car held the remains of the previous night. The familiar mental gymnastics had already begun.

"Can I throw it away?

Vodka? No, never.

Is there enough for another night?

No.

How much more do I need?

Enough to fill a small swimming pool, perhaps."

Your words though, they swept my legs out from underneath me.

"Thanks for letting me know."

What?

Sarcasm? Not your style. I check the time stamp on my message, heart sinking as the memory of the words I sent comes back to me. Middle of the night, drunken letter written to a near stranger. The man I pay to rummage around inside my head, to work out what poisoned my thinking and stunted my emotions. Kindness from another, for no apparent reason, always undoes me. It's my kryptonite. Leaves me weak-kneed and defenceless.

I read your words again. And again. Over and over. There'll be no drinking today after all. I could go visit you.

If I needed.

Do you know what you did with those few emailed words that day? I don't believe you do. When I saw you and thanked you for them, I saw the reaction in your eyes. Pleased, I think, but no idea? It's funny how the tiny gestures are the ones that assume giant proportions for others.

In the battle for the fixing that I say I want but can't commit to it is necessary to place you in the role of enemy. Twisting my thinking in ways that don't fit. Refusing to let me sink into the maudlin places. Does it exhaust you the way it does me, I wonder? The game? Or, well-practised at the art, is it no harder than pulling on your socks in the morning? Lacing up a pair of shoes?

For all your intellect and talent. For all the mental gymnastics and the games batting back and forth in your office, you beat me with a couple of typed sentences. Started the war in me. There could be some bloody battles.

Or there may not be. I have no clue.

2: What Happened?

I choose to believe I wasn't always this way.

Alcoholic.

Evocative of bleary-eyed men in trench coats clutching brown paper bags, most in polite society would avoid the word. Or the one who claims the epithet.

Addict.

Another word to send a delicate shudder down the spine of the genteel, the well-mannered members of society.

Yet, if that is my belief, where did I manage to gather up this gift? Where did the slide into the pit begin? A gentle downhill stroll at first, as I recall it. Speeding up towards the end as the gradient increased. The sides becoming near vertical and so slippery, impossibly hard to halt the final fall.

I am sister, child and grandchild of some compulsive individuals.

Lends weight to the genetic argument for this thing. I've heard it called; disease, perversion, sickness, feeble-mindedness. Lack of will power has been implied or selfishness. A part of me revels in these descriptions. I am a waste of time and space and resource – better go back to what I do best and self-destruct. Another part, disgusted, berates self. "Get a grip. Pull yourself together, woman. Sort your life out. Try harder to be better."

Crappy parenting and crappier biology conspired. The early discovery of the bottle, seductive and sultry. Calmed capricious moods and blunted painful emotions.

Discovering that my crushingly shy self could become the life and soul of the party with this social lubricant, "like me, love me, never leave me. . ." Such a needy child (and adult), but don't let it show. Never give the game away.

The subsequent discovery. The realisation that, drinking solo, my new best friend could numb the pain of being lonely and ashamed. Kill the sense that, somehow, I am not enough, impossibly bad, fundamentally flawed. For a short while at any rate.

I could stop at one drink in the early days if necessary. Never really understood why one would want to though. The aim with drinking always is reaching that elusive state.

Nirvana.

A rare moment of bliss, blink and you miss it. Or overshoot it waking later with blank space where memories should be.

"What did I do?

What did I fail to do?"

On occasion. "What was done to me?"

Harder and harder to find as one's drinking career progresses. The memory of that bliss, enough to keep me going back for more. In those early days anyway. Before the cravings kicked in.

3: Let Go and Let. . .

I smiled most of the way home thanks to the mental image from your crack about the hip flask and the church coffees. Did I tell you I hang with the Baptists? Imagine the carnage. I've never been that classy of a drunk, unfortunately. I'm more a vodka in the water bottle in the handbag kind of girl.

Both you and the psychiatrist asked about the tattoo. Those questions embarrassed me. I was thinking that you think the ink is a dumb thing to have done; what kind of idiot scars themselves to gain a few sober days. It can't possibly help one stay away from the drinking or help with the drinking thinking. The impulse with those questions is to deflect, not answer honestly – change the subject in the hope of seeming less stupid.

> *Which reminds me. You say the thoughts in my head are not the issue. It's just important to dial down the intensity of my reactions. Is that right? A friend said something similar a while back: "Doesn't matter about the thinking." I've always been quite fatalistic about the thinking though. Once the whispers start: "You aren't that woman anymore, she's crazy, you deserve to wind down." I tend to just cut out the middleman and accept defeat. Easier that way.*

The meaning of the inky date is tricky to pin down and can vary depending on mood or audience, but I'll have a go.

It was a line in the sand initially. I kept drawing lines only to rub them out again a day or so later. I couldn't think of any other way to make a promise that I wouldn't be able to wriggle out from under. There is a larger context to that belief though.

Our background is working class, mine and my husband's. You learn to drink when you can stomach the taste. He thought me posh when we met because I liked wine. I was at university at the time. A period best described Lemony Snicket style as "a series of unfortunate drinking related events." He saved me.

We drank wine together for years and moderated by only having the amount in the house that we were planning to drink that night. The dreams of a house with a wine cellar had to be abandoned, unfortunately. Sometimes we drank every night, sometimes weekends only. Occasionally sharing one bottle, usually two or three or more. He drove if we went out as he's always had this strange capacity to stop after the one glass or two.

He stopped drinking after some illness. I carried on and drank the wine bottle dry alone. Opening a second caused frowns so it was easier to add in nips from a hidden vodka bottle. Everyone's a winner. He told me I was mean when I was drunk. I didn't have a leg to stand on (literally) since I rarely remembered being drunk, much less mean.

Vodka can go down fast when needed. Family life shrunk drinking times to a couple hours here or there. I measured what I thought I could get away with in the time allowed and then would wake up a few hours later, on the living room floor (or beach, or wherever) with few memories and legs that disobeyed instruction. One drink never enough. Ice in a drink, or a glass even, were lost luxuries. Hard to tell exactly how much you drink when you can only judge by how many empty bottles you get rid of per week.

Finding places to dump empty bottles, almost as difficult as sneaking into the liquor store unnoticed in a small town. Each store visited in turn at different times of day to try to hide from the cashiers. The stench of shame breaking through the deliberately smart dress regardless. Always paying cash in a society where the debit card is king. Head down, scurrying out the door to my car. I imagine them thinking after me: "There goes another one."

Opportunist described my drinking career at this point. The job went. It was cramping my style. That and the fact that near-constant blind panic only quieted by the new best friend in the glass bottle influenced the concentration span.

I'd been talking to a friend about anxiety. A recently appointed pastor, once a drunk himself as it turned out. I was struggling to rationalise a faith telling me to "fear not" when I jumped at every shadow. Conversations took a confessional turn towards bottles in the handbag. He was joking when he said it. I was caught bang to rights. Maybe it was a God thing. He asked the questions.

"How often?

How much?"

Weirdly honest answers come in a church.

"When I can.

As much as I can.

Vodka, always vodka, she's the only one for me."

He told me a litre in one go would kill most folk. I tested his theory. It didn't but I scared some dog walkers on the beach the next morning. He took me to AA "to show me what I am" I still don't believe him some days. The tattoo helps to remind me what, a desperate control measure looks like. I couldn't get back the next week alone. But a little old lady picked me up from the gutter outside the front door and sat with me in a bus shelter for a while.

He told me to call once every day and tell him whether I'd had a drink. I agreed to text instead unless desperate. I mean, who does that kind of thing for someone else just because. He said he cared because God loves me. I go back and forth on that one too.

The next time I drank he called my husband at work. I called down unholy hell on him in response. He asked me not to forget the next day's text/call. At the time, I thought he was trying to help me not drink. Retrospectively, I suspect he was helping me to not lie. He called my husband every single time. The poor men barely knew each other.

I've rarely experienced such altruism in a person. There was literally nothing in it for him. He helped anyway. I'd probably do the same for someone else.

Probably.

That first time I stopped drinking I knew I was done. Dead is the only rock bottom I understand, and it wasn't that. I'd switched to gin since variety is the spice of life and alone at home with the luxury of ice, mixer and a glass. I felt indescribably happy. I hadn't touched the drink and I knew I didn't need to. Easy as. I called myself "fixed" but while I'm doing honesty the appropriate word is healed. I felt peace and I knew it was going to last and it did.

For a while.

Disappearing back into the chaos of your own head instead of letting go of the self, self, selfish thing is all too easy, unfortunately. This time to move the mountain I'm thinking I need a spade.

The inky date is nailed on skin tight as a reminder to let go of control daily, pray, and when all else fails, hold on and beg for mercy.

4: Is There Any Hope?

AA

I made it to the meeting again today. Last week I didn't speak, just sat there and shot through at the end. Some people remembered me and hugged me and stuff. I'm not a natural hugger, stand like a plank if I'm not forewarned of it and able to instruct the brain to make the limbs respond. I think I wear my terror on my face, but it's not an uncommon thing there. This week I knew I'd be invited to speak – you don't get missed out two weeks running, even in a big group. The record playing in my head was on a loop.

"Will you speak?
What will you say?
You can't speak.
Too many people."

I almost missed the request when it came . . . Panicked and blurted out "I'm terrified" instead of the words I'm supposed to say. At least it didn't cross my mind to run; I've run out on the meeting in my home town twice now. The shame of that mostly is what stops me from going back. I assume they'd be thinking, "Oh man, not her again. Drama queen."

The words were stupid. I was thinking I sounded like an idiot as I spoke, so I was already apologising for myself before I said anything and then I didn't know what to say. Once started though you have to continue, I've discovered, so I imagined I was telling a story. It's coming in handy, the storytelling. I told them that three months sober I had got so unable to bear the noise in my head that: bottle, knives, bush, police etc . . . and then a few months later I'd done it again. Only it was just the bottle this time since home alone, not cool. And my wrist. The inky date. If I get anxious in company I sit and scratch at it, like I can remove it, like it itches.

Several people offered me their numbers. I didn't know how to make my mouth say yes, please, thank you. Too scared. I hope I didn't make them think I didn't like them. Some people wrote numbers down anyway. I don't know how to call them. I haven't stored them in my phone even – too scary.

5: Bottle, Knives, Bush and Blood

And I've come full circle to the beginning in my thinking. The reason I get to spend so very much time in your company. Trying to see me the way you say I should. Always two steps forward and one back.

You were the one who called in the cavalry. What did you see, I wonder? I barely remember. I recall your face in the doorway when you came to collect me for our appointment that day. It seemed set. Stony. I knew in that expression that my doctor had followed through on his morning's threat to call you. To ask for a second opinion.

My poor doctor of the open-ended questions. "How are you?" What does one say when the reason for the appointment is to ask for a repeat of the medication that holds crazy brain at bay? "Fine" doesn't cut it. A lie that hangs in the air the second it is out. Possible answers travel through my brain. Each one brittle, shattering before the words can reach the mouth. I am struck dumb in front of him.

He tries again, rephrases the question, closed this time. "Are you safe?" The answer must have disturbed him. He asked my permission to make the call to you. I wondered to you at a later date whether I would have got away with it if I had answered in the negative to that request. You told me he was upset, worried, unsure and would have been making a call to somebody that day no matter what. We forget how we impact on those around us at times. I reflect that my appointment with him must have put a dent in his day. Did it dent yours too? I'm sorry.

You wanted to know how the hour-long drive had been. I said, "Fine. I followed another car." That was a lie. I felt guilty, but I didn't remember the drive at all. I got in the car to come to you and out of the car when I arrived. There was nothing in between. No noise at all in my brain. Suspicious silence from the choir.

You offered me a drink of water.

I was thirsty, but I said no.

You poured me one anyway. I've always thought you were part magician since then, you know. How did you know?

I held onto that glass like my life depended on it. Focused on the glass and the liquid within.

Listening whilst you called person after person. "I'm sorry. I'm really sorry." I remember saying.

"Don't be," you said. "It's my job."

No room at the inn that night. Sent home, sedated, to be collected the next day. Somehow I slipped the net. And lost my mind.

6: The Story I Told

There is a woman I know well. Six months ago, she tried to end her life. Most days she wishes she had succeeded. Three months before that she put down the bottle for what she hoped would be the last time. She will talk about it freely so long as you avoid asking why. She claims not to know and gets a little upset.

She will speak about the police officers who thwarted her plans, giggling about the one and only time she has been chased by a police car. Feet were never going to win over wheels! She will tell you about the police woman who stayed well past the end of her shift and the policeman who tried to give her his dinner. Her eyes will cloud over, however, at the thought of the nurse in the hospital who told her she should be ashamed for wanting to leave behind three boys and a husband. She could write you a book on shame, she thinks. The craft knife, hidden in her pocket, had disappeared by now, her escape route stolen or lost somewhere. By the time the sedative drugs wore off about a week later she will sadly comment that she had lost her nerve.

My friend found herself a few days later, parked up in the family car staring out at the ocean, attempting to answer her husband's question as to whether there was any hope in her. Defeated, she could think of nothing beyond God. Any hope to be had must have been with Him because it was utterly lacking in her.

My husband later commented that it was the most helpful thing said to him during that whole dark period.

7: Epilogue

I complain about you to my friends, you know. After an appointment.

Frankly, it still blows my mind that I have people in my life with whom I use the word "friend" at all. People that I have trusted with a little of my soul, who haven't chewed it up and spewed it back in my direction. People who just seem to like being around me. Without wanting something from me. It's a confusing concept.

You laugh when I tell you this. Say I'm funny. I initially tell you "no" but then accept the statement. The compliment.

This is what I complain about to friends. You force me into accepting the lovely ideas. And when I'm cornered into acceptance of one tiny shard of light, it's all you need to carry on. The next hour feels like forever as you go full force nine on the positivity. I walk out of your office reeling. On leaving the building I actually steady myself against a wall for crying out loud. The words have that much power over me. Your words are hypnotic. It's a talent. Did they teach you it in psych school, I wonder, or is it a natural gift?

My friends, laughing, carry on the joke. I feign disgust with them, stalking away. Real tears form though. When did I get this lucky? How do I even deserve this good of a life?

I ask you whether I'm better. You tell me I'm "well". You could be right.

Claire Hagan *is an ex Chemistry teacher turned librarian. She relocated to Whakatane from the UK four years ago with her husband and three boys. Reading has always been a passion of hers but her love for writing has developed only recently.*

Snow Umbrella — Artwork by Suzie Watt

Joy

Suzie Watt

The fading sun gradually begins to dip below the kauri. Its thick brown trunk leans stoically up against the rusty shed where it makes a slow groaning moan in the southerly winds, wrapping its arms into sleep. This was the problem with Invers. It got the sun early, then late in the evening its shadow slowly set across the wide plains to the south of Cooper's Point. The last light. It always seemed to be like a candle dimly diminishing until it put itself out. The hot wax, oozing into a glumpy glump.

* * *

Joy felt like she was swaying in the sea. Their last night together was boozy. It wasn't that they had always got together in sideways steps, but if they had been sober maybe the edge would have felt more like a widening crack that they would have avoided.

Hanging the tiny snow-caked squirrel up on the tree, her fingers feel numb. Where is he, for fuck's sake? The glitter of the decorations in her hands - dazzling specks of tiny metal flickers pulse up to her head. A small thump hits her heart. The boozy night again. Fuck.

"Morning, you're up early, Joy?" Doug says, with a stringy whistle through his mouth, the hole in his tooth extending her name into a wide arch. With a stoop to the right he turns, walks over to the window peering out at the first crack of light along the hill hump over on the Bates' farm. The cows ascending into a single long line, almost tipping off the edge into the ashen valley below.

"Hi, Dad, yeah, the cows needed checking over . . . old Minty has a nick in his hoof. Do you want me to call the locum?"

"Nah, love. I'll do it later, I have to go post a bill anyway. Where's Des?"

"She's down the creek. Something about the land sliding to Bennie's sheep. She thinks the next downpour will cause a flood."

Joy swallows, the woozy feeling again. Stumbling over the pile of glitter bulbs she gets up from the tree, pushes the plug in. The sequence bedazzles: a jumpy line of bobbles rapidly firing around the room. "I gotta go out, Dad." She turns, her fingers hovering over the plug. Leaving the lights on, she walks back down to the orange-tiled bathroom. The mirror isn't kind - her hair, a straw-tussled mess today. Blurry eyes. The white dotted curtain blows a gust into the room, whacking a little wooden owl into the bath with a thwack. Fuck, another southerly.

* * *

The carpark is full. Bingo in the community hall. A lunchtime chore. How did she get into this? What part of her ever wanted to be a part of such a hideous creation? It was Des. For the good of her spirit, she said. If only she could go back and drink another JDs. Where was he anyway? No txts.

"How's your mum?"

"Oh fine, she couldn't get in today. The creek . . . it's not great, three inches of rain in the night."

"7, 10, 16, 2 . . ."

"BINGO!"

* * *

The painted red line runs along the rim of the car. It gives off the impression that it can slickly speed along the asphalt. But no. The slow glide of the Holden edges its way to 55.

"So, where do you want me to drop you?"

"Oh, just in Cathedral Square. A girl from the hostel is meeting me. Thanks, Roy."

"Hmmm, well, I bet your mum ain't that happy."

"She will be, if I get in."

"Hmmm. Nursing aye. . ."

* * *

The room is stiff and still. What appear to be windows with long curtains hanging down to the bottom dusty floor give off an eternal sigh. Joy glances at her watch. It's ten to ten. Five minutes too long. Her legs have a red splotch from crossing them too hard. Her porcelain white legs. She swallows. Not so white after all.

The door swings open. A woman in a dark navy cardy, with a wide red skirt, pushes into the room. Her hair is grey, a slight red tinge. Her purple earrings dangle around her neck, swaying in rhythm – an African jive dancing towards her destiny.

"Joy? I'm Rowena Gibbons, the manager. How was your trip up?"

"Cold and long." Joy pauses, almost bites her lip. "The countryside is beautiful; I haven't been up here before."

"Joy, how old are you?"

"Seventeen."

"And your parents?"

"No."

"You wrote the letter four months ago. That makes it eight months or so now."

"Nearly nine. I say I have bad periods . . . so I eat more. Nick and I broke up. No one suspects anything."

"Right, well Lavender House has been running for five years now. It's fully funded by Presbyterian Support - although the government has given us some kindly donations. If it wasn't for local community help, such as knitting babies' clothes, bedspreads, we may not have done so well."

"How many people live here?"

"Well, at any given time usually five mothers and babies. And a guest room for adoptive parents. We try to limit our numbers so that our staff can have a 1:1 ratio. We have a room available now. Of course, you have to make the decision."

"I have."

* * *

His name is David. A solid name. Little fingers spread out then close shut as he takes his first gasps of air.

* * *

The high nor-west arch pushes around the bottom of the foothills in the northern distance. Heat simmers off the roads, almost making an oasis of palm trees appear. The Holden cracks, then sighs, reaching its crescendo along Memorial Ave.

"Jeez, so it wasn't for you, then?" Roy asks as he gazes at her, twisting his mouth almost into a knot. "I thought you would make a great nurse." He then pushes the pedal down, stares straight ahead.

Joy swallows. Her eyes steadily move across the sunline, watching the 747 as it rises up into the sky reaching for the white nebulous clouds. Taking some lucky person away.

"They had no slot for me. Too many girls applied. Maybe next year."

"Des will be stoked. That damn creek is causing her all sorts of problems. Struth!"

Suzie (Susanmary) Watt, *lives in Christchurch, New Zealand. She completed a BA from Canterbury University in Sociology and Music, following on with a Diploma of Computer Graphic Design from Natcoll/Yoobee. Suzie has just completed the MA (2018) in Creative Writing through AUT, gaining First Class Honours. This is her first piece of writing for publication.*

Full Moon Void of Course

Sandi Hall

The night is alive with wind, the yellow summer moon yet to be eclipsed by the earth's bulk. Have I heard a sound foreign to the murmur of the garden? The imminence of the eclipse has kept me awake, knowing that my atoms and shadows contribute to its shade.

Through next door's fence, Sarah, bright of eye through the slats that bound her world, gives a flurry of eager whimpers as I come out of my bedroom into the garden and look up to the vast mackerel-clouded sky. On the roof of the tool shed to my left, two ancient aluminium kettles rattle at the rough touch of the wind. There are spoons inside each kettle. At the wind's pull, both kettles and spoons jiggle, making angular sounds against the rushing voices of the garden, the soft clicks of flax and the long soughing of the fir tree. But I heard something other, or thought I did.

Is there a thief about? I hush Sarah and step forward, the wind wrapping its cool cloak around me. A lurch in the dark jolts my heart but it is only the hammock, wild in captivity between the fir and feijoa trees. Janet, daughter of my blood, familiar and alien as the domestic cat, brought it home three days ago.

Suppose there is a thief and he attacks me? My mind quickly obeys this directive, starring me in a suspense drama: blocky thug coming out of inky darkness, moon glint on steel, blood black on my round, pale arm. Instantly, my officious director takes over: "But it's not really dark, the moon is full, you can see quite clearly. And what do you mean, he strikes you and you do nothing? What are you?"

I am a female of the species known as human. The full moon once commanded me with all the power of the universe, and my womb obeyed. No more. Now I am an energy in a well-used body, facing the rock not the river and uncertain how to climb.

The kettles are now hip-hopping to the wind's tune. Janet has tied one end of two long black cords to each of their handles. The other ends circle the stems of the two large midlife marijuana plants growing below. "Viva vigilantes," I murmur, saluting my daughter's sagacity. A barely perceptible dimming turns my eyes upward, where clouds have scudded aside to show my and all the world's shadows edging across the rock that is the moon.

Sarah gruffs quietly as I move down the garden. The fir tree stretches up, the night darker under its spread. As if my arrival in the tree's umbra breaks some main current of the universe, the wind sighs into stillness. Sarah sneezes twice. I hear her terrier feet scrabble back up the steps. Ants move soundlessly up and down the tree's trunk, which I circle with my arms. Their little bodies are as cool as beads.

In the far distance, the wind or the sea roars and the spaces of me ache. I want to be opened and picked clean, to be taken to the bosom of an ageless force that never errs and whose beauty will never change. "Please," I whisper. The ants become still.

My body holds the tree or is the tree, the tango night and the dewy issue of the earth. Behind the shadow, eternity's thrush lands again on the moon, eroding it a little further with the yearly scratch of its clutching nails. Three four, one two, tell me, tell me, who are you?

I am a woman alive in her time, once a lover, once a mother, now a simple stepping stone. I feel my shape round out and flatten, feel tiny stones and mud below me. Water ripples past my shoulders, flowing over and behind me. Above, the eye of the moon half-closes, a sign of the times.

Later, all night's shadows thin to transient wraiths. Then comes dawn.

Sandi Hall's *writing includes seven published novels, several short stories, four plays, and some poetry. She is currently working (with whānau) on another play, this one about an overlooked Māori suffragist, Meri Te Tai Mangakāhia. And she is, with co-director Sophie Burns, about to launch her Cosmic Botanist trilogy into the Wattpad world.*

I'll Weather the Weather

[an old tongue twister]
Elizabeth McRae

what is this tether that I'm at the end of
can I find where it might start
were the chains ready to claim me at birth
is this the human condition
is this us knowing our place
no remission no stop no grace
must we *weather the weather whatever the weather*
whether we like it or not

in words we might find a distraction
where the mind can shuck off the shackles
they are there on the page on the tongue on the lips
to again stir the living with joy
come words and spatter my pages
let me tether you into a poem

Elizabeth McRae *has spent most of her working life as an actor. Skills for writing and acting are quite similar. Overacting and overwriting are to be avoided.*

Snakes and Ladders

Jacquie McRae

"Write a funny story this time," my teenage boy urges me.

I glance up from the kitchen table where I'm trying to write between the chipped crockery and piles of unpaid bills.

"I don't think life's that funny at the moment."

"It's a game, remember. Snakes and Ladders. You taught me that." He leans down and presses his lips to my cheek. "I gotta go. Write about that girl that used to stand on a beer crate and sing to the flowers in the garden."

I watch my youngest son bend his six foot three frame under the doorframe. I hold onto the smile he flashes me as he steps into the night. I fold it like a napkin and store it. "Be safe!"

I look down at the words I've typed on the screen. I read them aloud and they sound contrived. Somewhere between the space where I picked them and the place that I planted them, they withered. I hold down the backspace button. Does the world even need another story?

I stare at the white page and then flower girl leaps to the front of my thoughts. I see her waif-like face and spun-gold hair flowing down to her waist. Curious brown eyes stare at me and her wide smile shows the gaps between each of her teeth.

"Remember me?" she whispers.

* * *

"Mistress Mary." Nan calls out to me in the garden. "Come inside, it's getting cold."

I cup my hands around my mouth and yell back. "One more song, Nan, and then I'll come."

I turn back to the plants and wave my arms in the air like the conductor of a grand orchestra. Nan gives me the look and beckons me in. I step off my beer crate podium and tap each plant lightly as I wind my way back through my kingdom. I yank open the fly screen door and a gust of wind rushes in behind me.

"I think my science experiment is working, Nan. The plants are leaning towards me after only a few weeks of singing to them."

"It's more likely the wind is pushing them towards you. You'll catch your death from the cold standing out there half naked. Go put something else on and then come and eat your dinner."

I choose one of Nan's dresses from when she was young and slip the red sequin gown over my head.

"Going somewhere special?" she asks, looking at me over the rim of her glasses.

"I have a dinner date," I say, batting my eyelids at her. I take the newspaper that she's strewn over the table, and fold it so that the page with her half-finished crossword sits on the top. "Can we play cards after tea? I'll help you with the dishes."

"Maybe. I think you already owe me a window clean and a car wash. Don't you have any homework?"

"I did it on the bus and I owe you a window clean, car wash and a shoulder rub. I need a chance to win something back. My teacher said today that she thought it was wrong for a child to be playing poker. You'd be proud of me, Nan. I didn't tell her that I didn't care what she thought."

"Why did you tell her about the poker in the first place?"

"She asked how come I'm good at maths, so I told her."

"Well, there are things that are better left unsaid."

I get the cutlery and mats from the sideboard. A letter sits on the top and I recognise Mum's crazy scrawl.

"What's this?"

Nan turns to look at me as she's straining the peas and pours the boiling water over her hand.

"Shit."

"It's from Mum, isn't it?"

"Yes."

"When did it come?"

"A few days ago." She runs cold water from the tap over her hand.

"She's not coming to get me again, is she?"

"Not immediately."

"What? She can't just come and take me whenever she feels like it. I'm practically an adult and don't need her to look after me."

"I don't think you qualify at 12." Nan wraps a wet tea towel around her hand and lets out a long sigh. She places a plate of fried drumsticks onto the middle of the table. "Do you want some bread?"

I shake my head but avoid looking at her.

"Come on, eat up." She piles the chicken onto my plate.

"I'm not hungry." I pick at the chicken and shuffle the peas around my plate.

After dinner, Nan lights a small fire in the lounge grate. She takes the card table from behind the door and makes a show of flicking out the felt cloth that we use on special occasions.

"I'll play you to see who's going to peel all those peaches."

"I don't feel like playing. I'm going to bed."

"It's still light outside. Wait. . ." She walks to the Welsh dresser and stands on her tiptoes to get a carved wooden box from the top. She strokes the lid of it as she brings it to the table. Rolled up inside is a caramel cloth, tied together with a ribbon made of twine.

"What's this?"

"Moksha Patam."

"What?"

She unfolds the cloth and lays it out on the table before tipping some small shells from a silk pouch. "It's a Hindu game. It was my grandfather's from when he was a boy growing up in India."

I pick up a shell that's glazed like porcelain. My fingers glide over the smooth surface.

"Beautiful."

"It's a sea snail or a cowrie shell." Nan picks one up. "There was a time when people used them as currency. Tip it over up and you'll see an opening like a mouth. The ridges along the side would have been its teeth."

Painted on the middle of the cloth is a pattern of squares. Winding around the edges, deities dance amongst the jungle vines in blood red bloom. Gold ladders and serpents with open mouths link up some of the squares.

"How do we play?"

"I'll teach you as we go."

The snails rattle as she shakes them and then rolls them on the table. Four of them land with the hump sticking up, but two land tooth side up. "You count the tooth side." She taps two places forward.

I follow her lead and throw a four. I move and land in a square with a ladder. Fine black brushstrokes are at the base of it.

"What do these letters mean?"

"Each square has a different meaning. The one you're on refers to knowledge. It's the longest ladder on the board. You get to climb up the rungs."

She shakes and moves three.

"Is the winner the first one to the top, Nan?"

"Yes, but the game's more than a race for the top. It mirrors our life journeys. The ups and downs from our birth through till the final square, Moksha. It's the ultimate goal for Hindus as it represents freedom from sorrows and suffering."

I roll a one and then she rolls and lands on the head of a snake.

"The game's been played for over 2,000 years. It was used to teach people about values and vices. Good versus evil. This snake represents lying." She slithers down to the beginning.

"Maybe that's to do with Mum's letter." I stare at her. "You should've told me."

"I know. But, I was stalling for time."

"What did she want?"

"She wants to move closer. She says she's getting well."

"She said that last time and then she wasn't." I throw the shells and they all land teeth down. I pass them back without moving.

Nan jangles the shells in her hand for a long time."People do change. I think she deserves another chance." Nan throws a six.

I roll and point at the squiggles I land on. "I suppose you're going to tell me that these marks are for compassion?"

"No. It's resilience." She smiles with her eyes. "I knew you'd pick up on this game quickly. Whatever happens, Mary, know you'll be fine. Snakes and ladders, that's what life is."

Jacquie McRae *is a writer of short stories and novels with a Masters of Creative Writing with Honours. Last year she was a recipient of a Michael King Writers Centre residency and mentored on the Te Papa Tupu programme. She was included in the anthology Stories on the Four Winds and her first novel, The Scent of Apples, won an Ippy award and a White Ravens label.*

Easter 1983

Gillian Roach

Nana and Grandad brought us home
on the bus
our lives had changed

like when you swim in the sea
and when you get out
there are togs   sandcastles   jandals
but not yours

these are not your aunts and uncles
this is not your chilly bin
your gear a long hot trudge away

like when you wrap your arms around the legs
of the dark-haired woman in the white coat
but it's not your mother
she's over there   love

Gillian Roach *is an Auckland writer and recently completed an MCW at AUT. Her poems have been published in takahē and the Poetry New Zealand Yearbook. Gillian won the NEW VOICES – Emerging Poets Competition 2018.*

I Might Do Something

Olivia Spooner

"You have to come over, Elliot, straight away." Though Anne always thought long and hard before ringing her twice-divorced, often-depressed son, this was something she couldn't handle on her own.

"What's he done now, Mum?"

"Oh, Elliot, you won't believe me. You've got to come and *see*."

"Mum, I'm at work."

"It's six o'clock. Surely you can leave now? You have to come. I might . . . I might *do* something."

Anne waited. She leant into the pause. A pause was good. It meant Elliot felt the pull of familial responsibility.

Her son sighed. "Okay, Mum. I'll be there soon."

The phone rattled as Anne hung up, her hands shaking, her mouth dry.

What now?

She looked about the small kitchen. Nothing had changed – same wallpaper, same tired appliances, same stains on the bench, same everything – and yet it felt like someone else's kitchen now. *Despicable man.*

Jack had left the book he'd taken out of the library that morning on the table. Its title gleamed with a devil's grin. *Living and Thriving With a Disability*. What a joke. A cruel and twisted joke. Her husband hadn't "lived" a proper day since his stroke four years ago. And what about her? She'd been forced to go from wife, mother, friend, and valued member of the community to caregiver. And she hadn't once complained to anyone.

Anne wanted to burn that book. Take it outside, hold a match to it, and burn every single page. How dare he do this after everything he'd put her through. She picked the book up by its corner and placed it on the top shelf of the pantry underneath a tin of stale biscuits. *Try and reach it, you bugger. Just go ahead and try.*

Tears prickled in her eyes.

Sniffing and blinking, Anne wandered into the lounge, lowered herself into her faded floral armchair, and stared at the black television screen. It was quiet and still, her husband sleeping, no doubt peacefully in his bedroom. "I'll take a quick nap before teatime," he'd said. "Before I go online again."

Up until two weeks ago, he'd never gone "online" in his life. He'd shunned technology – mocked all those who used it. He'd said those idiots sitting in front of computer screens were wasting away, going brain-dead, letting computers do the thinking for them. As for kids these days, phones were brainwashing them, leeching humanity, teaching children too young to ride a bike how to miscommunicate with the world. He'd sat in that very armchair next to her, looked out at the street through the yellowed net curtain, and muttered his disapproval with everyone and everything.

Now Jack had a laptop on a specially designed table with wheels sitting beside his armchair. Instead of squinting out the window, he spent his time looking at his precious new screen, on the precious new laptop his precious new friend, Melissa – from the stroke support group Jack had suddenly joined – had got for him through some government-funded scheme. He acted foolish. Laughing and getting excited: the fingers on his left hand banging away on the keyboard like a toddler, his right arm hanging – forgotten, for once – at his side.

Anne stared at the small green light flashing slowly on and off on the side of Jack's laptop. She supposed she should get up and prepare some dinner, especially now her son would be arriving soon, hungry and expecting his mum to feed him. It wasn't like she didn't know what they were to eat: today was Wednesday, meaning today was sausages, and mashed potatoes, and frozen peas day. But Anne was resistant. She didn't want to cook. She didn't want sausages either.

Anne's eyes stayed fixated on the green light until movement at the edge of her vision made her look out through the net curtains to the footpath. Two elderly ladies were walking past. As her eyes adjusted, she recognised who they were and felt a flutter in her chest. Neither Alice nor Grace turned to look at Anne's house as they shuffled together down the street. Watching them slowly disappear from view was like watching the sun dip below the horizon.

Alice and Grace had been dear friends – possibly still were – yet Anne couldn't remember the last time they had spoken. Once a week, every week, for a good six months after Jack's stroke, they had popped round with a casserole or a cake, frequently together, but sometimes on their own. They'd stayed for a chat. More often than not it led to a gin and tonic or two. But as Jack soured, the visits became less enjoyable for everyone. He'd shout slurred, jumbled, hurtful words from the bedroom. Called Anne dreadful names in front of her friends. And they visited less and less. A natural progression, Anne supposed. She'd decided it was probably for the best they stayed away. The times after her friends walked out of the front door were the worst of the worst. Jack would turn acidic. He would demand she put him out of his misery. Couldn't she see that he would rather be dead than have her *shower* him? He never cried – he just became more morose with each year, more adept at loathing.

To think Anne had been the president of the local bowling club once. That she'd worked – well, volunteered, which felt better than work – at the hospice shop two days a week, and travelled there by bus of all things. On her own. Without her husband needing her to be anywhere.

Grace and Alice hadn't even glanced at her house as they went by. That was the bit that hurt the most. That was the bit that left Anne motionless as the room darkened.

When the doorbell rang, Anne jumped, knocking her leg against the coffee table. She leant forward and rubbed her shin, glad it was too dark for her to see the veins and splotches that seemed to be spreading over her thinned and greying skin like mould.

Hearing the doorbell ring again, Anne rushed to answer it, turning on lights as she went. She was tired and she hadn't cooked and she wished she'd never called her son. The fight had left her body, replaced by plain empty old age.

"Hey, Mum." Elliot stepped inside. "The old man asking for a shotgun again is he?" He embraced Anne like she was made of fragile china. What happened to those ferocious hugs she used to get when he was a boy?

"No, that's just it, Elliot." A breeze blew in from the open door, raising goosebumps on Anne's arms. "He doesn't even ask for a shotgun. He's changed completely since the car accident. I swear he's had some invisible knock to the head."

Anne didn't like to talk about the accident but it was clear to her the dreadful event had been the catalyst, the moment when her husband had undergone some kind of transformation. Or mutation may have been a more apt description. Yes, over the past few weeks, Jack had begun to slowly mutate in front of her.

"Well, that's a good thing, isn't it? Nice to know he's not thinking of blowing his brains out every few minutes."

"Elliot!"

"Sorry, Mum."

Elliot looked only mildly sorry as he walked past his mother and into the kitchen. He flicked on the lights and stared at the table. "Have you eaten?"

"No."

He opened the fridge and stared inside. "I'm starving," he muttered. "Missed lunch."

Anne pulled out a chair and sat down heavily, her head empty of words.

Eventually, Elliot sat opposite Anne, his mouth full of a bread roll he'd retrieved from the breadbin, filled with a large hunk of cheese. "So, what's up with Dad?" Anne watched the half-masticated food in his mouth as he spoke.

Now Elliot appeared to be listening, Anne didn't know where to start. “Since the accident, he’s started. . .”

“What happened to that boy, by the way?”

“I . . . I don’t know. I keep saying to Jack we should go and visit him in the hospital. I mean, it was nobody’s fault; we were just in the wrong place at the wrong time, but still. . .” Anne was lying. She felt total responsibility. She was the one driving the car. She was the one who hadn’t been able to swerve, or stop in time. “Your father says what’s done is done, that there’s nothing we can do for the lad. But that’s beside the point. I mean, it’s the right thing to go and see him, isn’t it?”

“Maybe.”

Elliot had finished the roll and was making himself another. Anne wasn’t sure if she was hungry or not. She did wonder how many bread rolls were left. Not that it mattered, but she’d planned to eat them for lunch the next day, with the pumpkin soup she’d made.

“There’s soup,” she said. “In the ice cream container in the fridge. You could heat up some soup.” What a relief to know there was something more substantial for her son.

Elliot stopped chewing. “What flavour?” he asked through his mouthful of gluggy bread.

“Pumpkin.”

“Oh.” Elliot looked crestfallen. “I’m not really a fan of pumpkin soup, Mum. You know that.”

Anne had remembered but only after she’d mentioned the soup. She liked pumpkin soup. That’s why she’d made it the day before, she recalled. She liked it and Jack didn’t. At her age, small things made a big difference.

“He’s getting up by himself now.” She sat straighter in her chair. The anger was stirring inside her again and she was determined to cling to it. “All those times when I had to drop everything and go running and now all of a sudden, he can get himself out of bed and into his wheelchair without me.”

“That’s great, Mum.” Elliot frowned. “Why do you make it sound like it’s a disaster?”

"It started the day after the accident. I was shaken, we both were, and I hadn't slept well. There was all this noise coming from his room but I just couldn't get out of bed. And then he appears in the doorway and he's *dressed*, Elliot. He'd actually managed to get his pyjamas off with only one arm and two pretty useless legs, and he'd put on trousers and a shirt – not that he could get the buttons done up, of course – but he was there, in the doorway, in his wheelchair, and he was. . ."

"He was what?"

Anne inhaled deeply. "He was smiling at me," she whispered before letting the air out of her lungs in a rush. "You wouldn't have recognised him, Elliot. It . . . it was. . ."

"Oh, Mum." Elliot reached across the table. "That's great."

It was the feel of her son's hand squeezing hers that caused Anne to burst into noisy tears. No one understood what she was going through, least of all her son.

After a while, Anne calmed down. Elliot heated up a bowl of soup and placed it in front of her with a flourish. "Eat up, Mum. It'll make you feel better."

"I expect he'll be awake soon," Anne muttered.

"He is awake. I popped my head in when I went to the bathroom. He said he'd be out in a minute. I'll cook him a couple of sausages while you sit there and eat."

She couldn't bring herself to thank him, just picked up her spoon and starting forcing mouthfuls of lukewarm soup – he couldn't even heat it up properly – into her parched mouth.

When Jack rolled slowly into the kitchen, his wheelchair caught Anne's elbow and sent a spoonful of soup splattering all over the black-spotted bananas in the fruit bowl. She'd been looking at them for several days trying to work herself up to making a cake.

"Sorry, love, still trying to get a hang of driving this thing with one arm." Jack reached up and patted Anne on the shoulder.

"It's fine," she murmured, unable to look at him. His touch on her body was still so unexpected and shocking she wondered how they had ever made love.

Oh, but they *had*, thought Anne, staring into the fruit bowl. Right up until two days before his stroke, at the ripe old ages of 73 and 75. They'd lain side by side enjoying an afternoon nap after a lunch with friends at the golf club. He'd kissed her lips and his hands had glided over her body and. . .and it didn't seem possible.

"I'm cooking you some sausages, Dad," Elliot said, smiling broadly.

"Thanks, son. That's very good of you. I was worried for a minute there I might be subjected to pumpkin soup."

Anne's spoon clattered into her bowl. There it was, evidence of his mutation. Gone was that slurry deep voice, sharper than cutting grass. It had been replaced with a tone others might have described as light-hearted. The man sitting there, engaging freely and without insult with their son, was not her husband. He was someone else entirely.

Later, Elliot perched on the arm of Jack's chair in the lounge and helped him set up a Facebook page. They were to be Facebook friends, whatever that meant. Anne watched them from the couch, listening to the way Jack was able to articulate words he'd been unable to even form a week ago. It was as if, suddenly, his stroke had been put into reverse. Anne wondered if he would start walking again soon. Maybe he'd regain full use of his right arm; what the heck, maybe he'd start to show reverse signs of ageing. Anything was conceivable, just as nothing made any sense. Anne closed her eyes and let herself drift off to sleep.

When she woke, she was still on the couch. Someone had stuffed a pillow beside her head to stop her tipping sideways, and she had a blanket over her knee.

"Hello, love," Jack said, patting her thigh. He was sitting next to her, a book open on his lap. "Elliot said to say bye." He closed his book and smiled. Anne recognised the front cover and remembered what she'd been thinking about before she fell asleep. Perhaps Jack was mutating so rapidly he'd managed to stand and reach the book himself.

"Elliot got the book down for me," Jack said, eyeing Anne closely – the way he used to do before she became his caregiver instead of his wife.

Anne blinked at her husband. They had to talk. She couldn't sit by anymore and watch him behave in such an appalling manner. "We need to talk about the accident, Jack."

Jack sighed and looked down at the book resting on his lap. "Look, Anne. It was difficult for you, I know. Terrible, really. But you have to admit it's worked for us."

Anne sucked air between her teeth. "What?"

"It was like some kind of shock treatment, wasn't it? I mean, I don't want to kill myself at all. Sure, I can't play golf, or tennis, or write letters to the editor the way I used to do, but we only get one life, Annie. I see that now."

Anne stared at her mutated husband. "Earlier today you went to the library with your *support* group." She spoke quietly, trying to keep herself under control. "You got out that book." Anne indicated towards Jack's lap.

"Yes, I did. It's great, full of ideas."

"I got it out, shortly after your stroke. I couldn't leave you home alone, but I knew you needed some sort of help, so I asked Elliot to watch you while you were asleep and I dashed to the library."

"I don't remember."

"You threw it at me. Called me a bitch. Said a life with a disability was no life at all."

"Well, those were dark days, Anne."

"Four years."

Jack's smile was uneasy, wary.

"We need to go and see the boy," Anne said.

"I'm not going."

"Why?"

"Because."

"Because why?"

"I'm just not, Annie. I've come so far –"

"Then I'll go on my own." Anne flung the blanket off her knee and charged out of the room.

"I was hoping you'd help me into the shower, love," Jack called, his words as clear as a man in the prime of his youth. "If it's not too much trouble."

* * *

Outside the main entrance to the hospital, several people propped themselves against the wall, smoking. Some wore hospital gowns and plastic slippers. They looked down at their feet, squinting as they sucked and blew. Inside, the foyer was dark, yellowed, and sick-looking. It smelt of Chinese food and rotten lemons. Anne asked at the information desk for directions.

For ten minutes, she stood outside the locked doors to the children's ward until a nurse – no doubt thinking Anne was someone's doting grandmother – let her in. "Who are you after there, lovey?"

Why, as you grew older, did everyone address you more and more with variations on the word love? Darling, lovey, lovely, love. Was it so obvious: that desperate need for affection?

"Ah, his name's Oscar," Anne stammered, sweat trickling between her breasts.

"Room 12, my darling, right over there." The smiling nurse pointed down the corridor, then walked into a room. Glancing in behind her, Anne could see a small girl with a head of blonde curls lying on a bed. She was propped up facing the door, and grinned at the nurse as she entered. She looks fine, Anne said to herself. I can handle this.

The door to Room 12 was closed. Anne knocked gently and adjusted her handbag on her shoulder. A middle-aged man opened the door. His body looked crumpled up, like he'd recently been squashed inside a box.

"Hello," she said, her voice cracking. "I'm sorry to disturb you, but I felt, well, I wanted to visit and see how the boy – I mean, Oscar – was doing. I really don't know if it's appropriate I'm here, but I am

. . . and . . . and I am sorry, really, I am so terribly sorry." Anne's hands clung tightly to one another.

The man stepped back and opened the door wider. "Please come in. Oscar's asleep at the moment, but you're welcome to . . . it's very kind of you to visit."

Anne liked the sound of the man's voice. It was soothing, calm, and monotonous. She guessed he was the boy's father – he looked like a father – patiently standing there, resigned to whatever came next.

The room was dim, blinds pulled down over the windows. A smell Anne immediately disliked wafted towards her. It reminded her of the underneath of their house where they kept the lawnmower and Jack's tools. Stale and earthy, slightly sour. Mechanical hiccups came from a tall narrow machine beside the bed. As a red light flashed, there was a slurp and a fast double beep.

Though the light was poor, Anne could see enough. The boy had a bandage wrapped around his head. His eyes, nose, and mouth poking through the white gauze looked like plants sprouting from the ground. Tubes ran from his nose, mouth, and arms. A thicker tube stuck out of his heavily bandaged chest and ran down into a big container half full of some kind of yellowy mucous laced with blood.

Anne's eyes travelled down the boy's body. She made an "oachh" sound and fought to swallow the vomit at the back of her throat.

Half a leg. He had a thigh, somewhere under those bandages, but the rest of the leg – the knee, the shin, the ankle, the feet, the toes – was missing.

"Oh no," Anne groaned, inadvertently reaching up to grab the father's shoulder to steady herself.

"It's okay. Comes as a shock. You're not the only one." The man patted her hand where it pressed into his shoulder.

A woman appeared from the shadowed corner of the room, mercifully blocking Anne's view of the boy. "Who exactly are you?" the woman asked, crossing her arms. It was clear to Anne this was the protective mother. Protective and terrified.

"I'm the driver," Anne stammered. "Of the car. I should have come sooner, but my husband's had a stroke, and it's hard for me . . . for me to get out."

The father took a step away from Anne and her hand slipped off his shoulder.

"What are you doing here?" the woman hissed.

"I'm sorry. Jack said we shouldn't come, but I thought . . . I'll go. I'm sorry. I'll go."

"It's okay," the man said, his eyes flicking to his wife, then back to Anne. "Thank you. I know it must have been hard for you to come."

"Oh, you have no idea *how* hard. But I had to. I had to say sorry to your boy."

"I can tell you now, you are the last person he wants to see." The woman looked freezing: white and shaking; it was as if a southerly gale were blowing through her.

"I understand," Anne said. "But, will you tell him I came by? Tell him I think about him all the time and that I wish . . . that I wish him a speedy recovery."

What Anne wanted to say was that she wished she could take his place. She wished it so much she ached. She was old and could do with the rest. Others would have to take care of her for a change. How lovely that would be. Half a leg, for Anne, would be no disability at all.

As she backed out of the room, the boy opened his eyes and stared straight at her. She shuddered. That look. It was the same one her husband, Jack, had given her every time he demanded she bring him a shotgun.

Eyes down and moving as fast as her wobbly legs would let her, Anne left the children's ward, took the lift to the ground floor, followed the exit signs around corner after corner, until she finally made it to the main doors. Head still lowered, she found her car, negotiated the car park payment, and drove slowly out of the exit onto a four-lane road thick with commuter traffic.

Driving past the small group of shops near her house, Anne spied

Betty's Bar. She made a quick U-turn and parked outside. The bar had been open for about a year. Anne had mentioned it once to Jack. She told him a trendy new place had opened up down the road and that it was permanently full of young people. She'd mentioned it as a way to break up the silence between them, not because she had an opinion about it, or wanted one from him. Certainly not because she wanted to go there.

What struck Anne all those times she'd driven past was how the younger generation seemed so full of *life.* They were always so quick to smile and laugh and throw an arm over one another's shoulder. Everything they did looked so effortless it seemed cheap.

Anne wanted a gin and tonic with lots of ice. She walked up to the counter, and waited patiently behind a young man who reeked of aftershave and who kept pulling his phone out of his pocket, glancing at it, and putting it away again. Finally, Anne managed to make an order.

The bar was stuffy and noisy. Anne risked a quick look around as she waited for her drink. She was by far the oldest. There were no seats anywhere, not even at the bar.

Jack hasn't mutated, Anne thought. *He's traded his soul with that boy. Traded selfishly, like a bitter, greedy old man.*

"Despicable," Anne said loudly.

No one turned her way.

She *would* find a way to give back to the boy what her husband had stolen.

Standing at the bar, she drank her gin and tonic. Then she ordered another . . . and another. . .

Olivia Spooner *is a writer who believes in the power of words to change lives. She encourages others to share their stories, nurture their creativity, and read good books. You can follow her writing journey and check out her credentials at oliviaspooner.com*

**Tram Stop: Palackého náměstí, Prague
— Photo by Garth Powell**

Garth Powell *is a photographer and visual artist born in New Zealand and living currently in the Czech Republic. He makes pictures primarily in monochrome, focusing on the balance between the truth and the obscure or abstracted.*

Argento and Raffaele

Michael Giacon

Michael Giacon *is a poet, songwriter and performer. Born and raised in Auckland, he is from a large Pākehā-Italian family. He has been published in brief, A Fine Line, Fast Fibres, and Fresh Ink 2017.*

We kiss by the fire, me shouting
a translation to your heart
red marble shining, snow outside
embers ash-white on a darkened world.

In time I'm in sunshine pricing minutes
where distance waits like a thief to steal
strength from our separation. The mood
you made the music for, it's here, ready
to call through mountains you go to
on Sundays, alone.

I had meaning on my side, I was special
and I missed the sounds you found.
In my lack of language you heard echoes
in what I tried to say. I never got to go
with you that Sunday to mountains
that spoke so clearly.

Late autumn, early spring, a bitter wind.
Like our winter I'm before the past
and maybe the modest fire, perhaps
the undecided day saw me too certain
as I tried to embrace your heart
red marble shining, ash-white
to your dark world.

Let Me In

Feby Idrus

There was a knock at the door. Banging, really; that's all that would get through the jet airplane's thick plug door. The pilot was standing at attention outside the cockpit as I walked down the aisle to disembark. He saluted.

"It's been an honour to fly you home, ma'am."

I saluted in return and smiled.

"Thank you," I replied.

He was the first flesh and blood human I had spoken to in 12 full months. All the other humans I'd talked to that year had only been images that had been fragmented, transmitted and reconstituted on my video monitor on the Space Station. Until him, I had only been talking to pixels.

I walked down the steps from the jet to the airbase runway, greeted by a cluster of NASA staff and cheers. Director Krenek shook my hand. His smile was tired but genuine.

"Welcome home, Commander Jackson," he said. "It's good to s–"

A child squalled. I looked around. That little wriggly toddler was in – Justin's arms. My husband Justin. But then that must mean . . . that was my baby. The baby I left behind to go into space. Was that . . . my child?

I started to cry.

* * *

There was a knock at the door. I went to open it but Justin beat me to it.

"Let me do that," he said. He'd been saying that a lot.

Another delivery of flowers.

"To Commander Antonia Jackson. Welcome home. You are a true inspiration to us all. Warm wishes, the Harvard Alumni Association," Justin read out from the attached note, holding the bouquet to his side like a baby.

"Just put them over. . ."

Justin ignored my finger, pointing towards the dining room table, and took the flowers into the lounge, to join all the other bouquets from associations I barely knew and didn't really care about. He lay the flowers down on the sideboard by the window, then noticed the piles of folded laundry on the coffee table. "You?" he asked, gesturing.

"Yeah. Trying to keep myself occupied."

"You don't have to do that," he said, warmly. It was like he was talking to an overly helpful hotel guest.

"Justin. It's my laundry. In my house. It's fine."

He leaned in and kissed me, only on the cheek. It felt strange being in his space. "Yeah, I'm sure you missed folding towels for a year," he teased.

"Actually, I missed folding towels that didn't float away from me," I said.

Later, I opened the linen cupboard to put away a pile of towels and found I'd folded them wrong. Or, at least, I'd folded them differently to all the other towels in the cupboard. Had Justin just started folding them differently, or had I. . .forgotten? How had Justin folded them? I unfolded one of his, tried to emulate it in mine. My towel sat askew, corners akimbo. So, I thought, towels did float away from you here, too.

* * *

There was a knock at the door. "Are you ready?" a muffled voice called.

I answered yes and pulled my hospital gown closer around me. The doctor, a pimply young man I didn't know, entered and launched into the usual preamble about this being a normal examination that every astronaut has after touching back down . . . I tuned out. I had heard it all before, in my pre-mission check-up.

I was put through my paces like a horse competing in dressage. The doctor who had come in was my pilot through this process, but other doctors and nurses came in periodically to observe, make notes and consult. I recognised none of them. How was this possible? My last mission, and my pre-mission check-up, hadn't been that long ago. The same protocols were being undertaken, by people doing the same roles. But all the roles had been recast. My workplace swirled with unknown faces. My life at NASA was a movie that had been rebooted without consulting me.

I got home and talked to Justin about it. He laughed, even though I wasn't amused. Then he kept on feeding Antonia. I watched them together like I was watching them on a movie screen. Observing. Not engaging.

* * *

Knocking. Justin called, "Can you get that, please?" through the open door of the downstairs bathroom, where he was bathing Antonia before bed. I put down the wet plate and dry dishtowel, went to the front door, opened it, and immediately wished I hadn't. Wished I'd remembered the precise details of what my Earth life had been before I left it to go into space.

There she was. Jess, at dusk. A precise detail I had made muddy in my head but whose corners were swimming into HD focus now. "Hi, Tonia," she said. So tall, blonde, impassive. A queen. A wall to break yourself on. Or maybe that's how she saw me.

"Hi." I had never been articulate, but a year in the blackness of space had stolen what little eloquence I had harvested over the years, and now 'Hi' really was the best I could do when confronted.

"I'm sorry," she said. "I know you don't like me just turning up at the house. He's here, isn't he? Of course he is."

"He's bathing Antonia."

"Okay. I don't need to come in or anything," she said, and I saw that she meant it but hoped I'd insist on welcoming her in. I couldn't, of course. I could not let her in.

Jess shook her hair back. There she was again, now that cloud of insecurity had glided away. The eclipse had passed, and she shone her stark light out as before. "I just wanted to say that I'm glad you're home safe and I think it's amazing that you went. Truly amazing. It must have been extraordinary."

Every morning on the Space Station, I would go to a window and look out at the view. The view of Earth. That vast blue globe, like a luminous pearl in black oil, shining, shining. And beside it, the lamp-like moon. That view expands you from the inside. I became a woman who contained multitudes. Others whined about the loneliness of space, saying humans need social interaction, that they need company. Not so. Who needs humans when you have galaxies blossoming inside you to keep you warm? A year in space, and now my heart twinkles with the constellations.

"Yes," I said, when I returned to present day Earth, and to Jess. "It was extraordinary."

That night before bed, I checked my phone. Jess had texted me – probably soon after she left the house. "Does he know about us?" it read.

I listened to Justin's deep sleeping breaths. No, I had not told my husband about the woman I had an affair with. The woman with whom I'd considered running away. What kind of question is that? Why would I tell? There are some things you can't be honest about with your husband.

* * *

"Knock, knock," Justin said. He tapped a knuckle on my temple. "Penny for your thoughts?"

I'd forgotten he did that, and that it could be both endearing and irritating. I continued looking out the window, at the full moon. She was pregnant with light. "I've seen the moon up close," I said.

"Do you miss being up there?" he asked.

I said nothing. Just kept gazing on her.

Quietly he said, "We missed you."

That afternoon I tried to play dolls with Antonia. I walked my doll up to the door of Antonia's dollhouse.

"Knock, knock," I said, tapping the doll's hand on the door. "Can I come in?"

Antonia looked at me blankly. Who are you again? she said with her eyes.

They didn't miss me. They were a closed unit. They had each other for company. I observed this and felt only an echo of pain. Seeing them was like seeing an affecting story on the internet. Oh yes. That's sad. Keep scrolling.

* * *

I texted Jess. "I don't belong here. I feel like I'm an alien." Knock, knock. Let me in.

One evening, while Justin bathed Antonia, I went to put away some just-washed teaspoons, opened the top drawer on the left of the sink and was greeted by – spatulas. Tongs. Plastic slotted spoons. Isn't this where the teaspoons went? I opened the second drawer down. Tea towels. Spare oven mitts. Where did the spoons go? I couldn't remember.

I stood in Walgreens, in an aisle of cold air, presented with four long rows of cheese. Monterey Jack. Pepper Jack. Humboldt Fog. Velveeta. For God's sake, I just needed a block of cheese, any cheese. But what kind of cheese was I supposed to get? I would have texted Justin to ask but he was. . .not happy with me. ("Can you at least *try* to help with the baby?" he had snarled.) Earth had too many things. Too many choices.

I lay beside my husband in the middle of the night, awake. Two strangers together, in our marital bed.

I looked out the window in the middle of the night and considered the moon. In my hand I held my phone. The reply from Jess blinked up brightly at me. "Then where do you feel you belong?" it read.

* * *

I knocked on his door. Krenek opened it. I sat down opposite him and explained. His eyebrows lifted. "Are you sure?" he said. "I think you need more time."

"I don't," I replied.

* * *

There was a knock at the door. Banging. It was Justin. I let him bang, even though I knew it was useless and I would have to open the door eventually, and when I did the fight would be bad. "Another mission?" he would say. "You just got back and you want to leave again? What about Antonia? What about me? Did you even think about. . ."

I turned off that voice in my head. I was busy looking at the moon.

There was another knock on the door. And I climbed out the window. Stood in the garden with flowers cooling my feet, gazing up at the full moon above me. "Don't worry," I whispered to her. "I'm coming home."

Feby Idrus *is a music teacher, freelance musician, and arts administrator. Her work has been published in takahē and Headland, and the anthology Horizons 2. She lives in Dunedin. Find her on Twitter: @febyidrus*

Losing Our Words

Alexandra Fraser

Alexandra Fraser *is an Aucklander, a prizewinning poet who has been published in many magazines and anthologies. She is a graduate of the AUT MCW and her second poetry collection, Star Trails, will be published later this year.*

the poem speaks to the page
sometimes shouts

inky saliva spray
a splatter of syllabic

wood pulp   chewed
by wasps

remoulded to object   blank
structure   waiting surface

to hold tight our words
for a few days years

till the wet dog of rain
or the incinerator flame

the slow decomposition
in the city dump

deconstructs texts to particles
pigments and lignin

fired to ash on the wind
rotted to landfill

rain falls
a few drops a thousand

the world's words
drowning

Extract from

The Night Bus

Lincoln Jaques

It was closing in on half-midnight, my last city run of the shift, and I was looking forward to getting home to a cold lager and a rubbish movie, when the kid they sent to kill me boarded my bus.

He didn't swipe his card and he didn't drop any notes into my tray. And I didn't argue with him: it wasn't any use arguing; he was there to do a job and for either or both of us this was going to end badly.

He'd got on near the casino and I guessed he'd been there most of the evening, due to the stink of beer and cigarettes that followed him in. I imagined he'd been going through it all in his mind, over and over what was going to happen, what he'd say, how he'd face me off, like an Olympian who needs to visualise each move, each stroke, each step before a big event. He could've just shot me through the open door – nice and simple, something I probably would've done in the old days – but it seems he wasn't that stupid. There were a few passengers already on the bus, and a small crowd gathered at the bus stop where he waited for me.

After he played the pathetic game of not paying a fare and pretending not to know me, he swaggered down the aisle and sat on the rear seat, smack in the middle, so he had a long, unobstructed view down the aisle in the event if I tried to make a dash for the open door he could, if he was very fast, pull his pistol out and shoot me part way.

But I wasn't that stupid either.

And if he knew anything about me, he'd know that. And I knew he knew that about me by the way, underneath his swagger and his beer breath and his handgun that bulged underneath his red-chequered bush jacket, his face gave away his fear. Despite only glancing at him briefly when he boarded, I'd taken in his details. He was young, early 20s, unshaved, a handsome face, brown-skinned, of Middle Eastern descent, maybe, or perhaps Indian. More Indian, come to think of it. His shoulders sagged, which let him down a bit. But that may have been due to his bending over slightly to hide the gun. What with his bush jacket and his dirty boots, he could have just walked off a dairy farm in the Waikato.

I moved the bus off and swung her out into light traffic, down past the shining hotels and the brimming bars with fancy, ingenious names and the late-night lights of the City Star, the Forte Convenience, Circle K, the Seven Mart, their paranoid owners sitting behind caged-in counters like bank tellers from the Wild West. Then the streets emptied some more and the yellow streetlights flowed over the asphalt and above me rose the commercial skyscrapers – Zurich Insurance and the Vero building and Air New Zealand and other banking and financial corporations – and all amongst those peeked the colossal Metropolis apartments, shabby and lean and worn against the new endless sleek glass faces. Then I slid past the Britomart Transport Centre and the surviving colonial façade of the Old Customs House and I left behind the business district and came out into a new development of apartment blocks hugging the waterfront like pins stuck in a cushion. Then I was curving around the marina where all the yachts and pleasure boats swung back and forth on the crescents of gentle waves. Then over the bridge, and I looked out and saw the almost full moon, a washed out imperfect circle against the clear, blue-black sky, its white light reflecting off the dark water as if someone had placed a giant, silver sword on its surface, its sharp point directed straight at me.

All this time I kept glancing in the rear-view mirror, checking the killer's position, seeing if he moved – if he dared move – from his seat. But all the way he sat silently, looking down at the smudged floor, hugging himself, fingering his gun beneath his jacket. After the bridge I started dropping people off. I switched the destination board over to N.I.S. – Not In Service – and finally I pulled into the depot and carried on behind the main set of buildings where they maintained the buses, as I did every night after my shift, as if nothing was any different, as if I didn't still have one passenger left sitting on the back seat, sweating, with a gun concealed against his guts. I pulled the bus in next to a row of buses. I killed the engine.

I reached over to kill all the lights too, when he said, "Don't turn off the lights. Leave the inside lights as they are."

I didn't say anything. I left the lights on.

"I want the lights left on. I can't see you without the lights. And I want to see you. I want to look at you and see you in all your detail, in case I need to shoot you dead."

After a long silence, I said, "Can I get up out of this seat? You can't shoot me from there. I'm partially hidden by the wall."

He considered what I said for a minute. Then he pulled out the pistol. He pointed it at me. "You step out of there real slow, man. Real slow, as if you're stepping on eggshells. As if you're walking through a minefield. And you face me, man. In the light, where I can see you."

I raised my hands and stepped out of the driver's compartment. I turned to face him. He got out of his seat and walked about halfway down the aisle.

He said, "You Joshua? Joshua Wallace Hamnet?"

"That's me. But I hate that name, so don't use it too much."

The end of the pistol shook in his hand. He kept grasping it, as if his palm was slippery with sweat which I'm guessing, by the looks of his face, it was. I took a step forward, to test him.

"You stand there real still, Mister," he said. "Real still now. They'd rather I bring you in alive, but dead is just as good. But alive I get paid more. And I need the cash."

"There's more honest ways of making a living," I said.

"Like driving a bus? Like you? Hell, you don't look so tough. They said you were tough. They kept saying you were the best. But I don't see no skills. Just a dried-up bus driver."

"What do you need the money for?"

He paused, blinked. Contemplated whether or not to open up to me. "My girlfriend, she's preggers. Well, Justine ain't exactly my girlfriend, she's just a girl I know. But now we're connected. And her old man is scary. Scarier than you, even. I need the money. They said they'd pay me. The sort of money they offer, you don't earn that in a year of washing dishes."

"Who are they?"

"Oh, no, you don't. You don't get that information outta me."

"You wash dishes?"

"What?"

"You said, you don't earn that sort of money in a year washing dishes. Where do you wash dishes?"

"Quit the small talk!"

"Hey, I'm on my last legs. You got me. It's probably better if you kill me now. Small talk's all I got."

He looked at the gun. Then he looked at me. Then he looked at the gun again.

"In a place uptown. An Indian restaurant. The Taj Mahal. You heard of it?"

"Sure. That's a nice place. I can taste their onion pakoras now. Say, a man's entitled to a last meal."

"I wish I could help you, Mister. But they hired me, they already gave me an advance, and I gave that advance to Justine. So I ain't letting you go."

"Fair enough, so what do we do now? These lights in here have been blazing these past five minutes. Anyone passing can see us. They may have seen you. Our faces are clearly visible. If there's anyone still up in the office, they'd have seen us too. Besides that, there's a security guard on duty. He could come wandering down here to do a check any minute now."

He thought about this for a few seconds, before saying: "All right. Okay. Here's how it's gonna happen. You're gonna go ahead out the door and I'm gonna follow. Remember I've got the gun on you. Nice and slow."

I already had the front door open and, still with my hands in the air, I walked down the steps and out into the night air. The evening was warm, the sky still clear, the moon still almost full but perhaps it looked a little less full now.

"You got a car?" he asked.

"Sure have. A nice car too. Took me years to restore it. Over there, parked by the bins."

"Holy! A Triumph Herald. It's immaculate!"

"A '68 model. Not many around now." I could tell he was genuinely impressed, and I was impressed that he was impressed. The kid was growing on me. I almost felt sorry for what I had to do, if he got stupid. We walked over to the Herald. Its bonnet was painted white, with a thin white stripe going down either side, a light shade of blue covering the rest of it. It looked like a dart, like an arrow shooting through the night.

"Well, there it is," I said. "What now?"

"You drive, and I'll direct you. No funny business now. I got this gun and I'll use it."

"I never thought for a moment you wouldn't. Say, I just thought though, I'm down five bucks."

"What?"

"I'm down five bucks. You didn't pay, when you boarded. Now I'll be down five bucks in my float. I've never been down, not one cent. They won't be happy with me."

"Well . . . well, I'm sorry for that, Mister, but I ain't got one red cent to my name. I lost the last bit of cash I had on the pokies. And anyways, you may not see tomorrow, where you're going."

"No," I said, rather sadly. "No, you're right. This is my last night. My last sky. My last moon. My last run out of town. And now I'll be down five bucks in my float and that will destroy a perfect record. Say, can I have a last cigarette, before we get in the car?"

"No, get in the car. Let's go."

"Come on, kid. You seem okay. You're smart. Well, apart from leaving the lights on in the bus. But you're doing well."

The kid hesitated. He looked me up and down. His eyes darted around the empty depot. The lights hanging over the parking bays caught his dark eyes and I could see he was breaking.

"Okay. One cigarette."

"I'm going to have to reach into my pocket and get them, unless you have some?"

"No, I ran out."

I dug two fingers into my front pocket and took out a packet. I slid two cigarettes out and offered him one. He reached forward. I dropped the cigarette and he stupidly bent to pick it up. I grabbed him by the collar with one hand and with the other clasped the wrist that held the pistol. I twisted the wrist and he let out a yelp and the gun fell into the gravel. He started to retaliate but I threw his torso around and wrapped his arm up behind him and rammed his head against the side of the steel bin. In the thin light, I saw a spurt of blood and he went limp, but not unconscious. I was careful enough not to go too far. He buckled onto his knees.

"Don't kill me. Please, Mister!" He started to hyperventilate.

"Okay, kid, relax. Just breathe. Deep breaths. Now, I'm not going to ask who sent you or any details like that. Because I can guess who that is. As I said, you seem a good kid, but you've now got yourself mixed up in deep shit. So I'll let them take care of you. But I want you to do one thing for me. Go back and tell them it's not going to be that easy. Tell them if they want me, they should try harder, and not send some amateur wet-nose with a pregnant girlfriend to do their dirty work. You got that?"

His head shook under my grip.

"Now go."

I released him and he staggered away a few steps. I took a few $20 notes from my pocket and threw them on the ground. "Get yourself a taxi."

I watched as he silently retreated, clutching his head, out of the depot and into the night. Then I picked up one of the discarded cigarettes and lit it. Took in a deep lungful of tobacco. Next, I picked up his handgun and walked over to the Herald. I got in the driver's side, threw the gun into the glovebox, started the engine, which purred like a contented cat stretched across a warm couch, threw it into gear, and a joy sprang up inside me as the wheels skidded across the loose metal on the ground and I shot past the bus, its inside lights still ablaze.

Lincoln Jaques *is a UK-born Aucklander. He holds a Master of Creative Writing from AUT, and his work has appeared in PNZ, JAAM, Southern Ocean Review, Spin, Fresh, and Shot Glass Journal (US), as well as the 2018 and 2019 Poetry New Zealand Yearbook. He has a flash fiction piece included in the April 2019 themed edition of Flash Frontiers.*

Mount Cargill from Otago Harbour – Woodcut by Manu Berry

Manu Berry *is a Dunedin printmaker. He co-runs a family art gallery on the Otago Peninsula with his mother, stepfather, and sister, who are all practising artists. Manu has exhibited in galleries around New Zealand, including several public galleries in the South Island. Recent projects include illustrations for an upcoming bundle of poetry collections by 6 New Zealand poets, and for a doctoral thesis: Manu: A Comparative Study of Polynesian Narratives by Raphael Richter-Gravier.*

New Year

Paul Hewlett

Paul Hewlett *is a poet, novelist and public relations consultant based in Auckland. His work has appeared in the NZ Herald, Turbine and The Yak, and on National Radio. His first novel, Moonzoo (fictionland, 2003), was one of New Internationalist's books of the year.*

New Year

the house cracks
its wooden joints
as the heat subsides
my feet ache delightedly
from running on sand
lightning flickers
above the dry hills
a three-quarter moon
waits for clouds to pass

as my children sleep
I think what have I to say to them
but sunshine
what embrace
but the whitewash
of the waves
what wisdom but
drying in the sun
what art but playing
ukulele as the sun sets

someone breaks out the cards,
you're scum, dad.

The Game

Henrica Schieving

The day started with the dead cat. A stiff, curved, horseshoe tabby. The misjudged dart across the avenue. The blur of fur under the right wheel of the Ford Anglia. The small thump. A last beat of the heart.

I saw it first. I burst into the staffroom stuttering with shock.

"Plllllease, Miiiiss, aaa cccat, Mmmiss." My nose was running, my bony-scabbed knees encrusted in dirt from yesterday.

All of us senior children stood at the fence railings and looked on as Mr McIntosh held the wooden apple box with reverence as he crossed the avenue. He pulled up his breeches, crouched on his haunches, and lifted the cat into its temporary coffin. The gate clanged after he walked through. The show was over and the seniors scattered to their classroom.

Word was it was Rosemary's cat from across the road. Mr McIntosh walked with the box through the school gate towards her house.

Rosemary was a new five-year-old in the junior class. She had rags in her hair each day. On Sundays, shiny ringlets bounced like springs on her walk to church. She was the first-born of her family and so her dresses were always clean and ironed, her socks white, and her leather shoes polished. Her nose had an upwards tilt and it made her appear as if she was always pretending to be a princess.

The ticking clock and scratching chalk were loud in the room as the maths lesson wore on. My book had ink blobs where I had taken too long to work out the sum. I looked with longing out of the window toward the field.

Miss Sullivan glared at me. "Albert! You should be on the second set by now. Pay attention, young man! Also! I believe it was *you* who cleaned the dusters yesterday? You obviously need more practice. And, use your handkerchief, *please*!"

I fished a bunched-up hanky out of my pocket and I wiped it across my nose and cheek. A trail of snot started to dry.

The bell rang for morning break. Miss Sullivan dismissed the class and 25 wooden chairs scraped on the floor.

The game at the bottom of the field started at each break as if it had never stopped. Everyone stood in the place they were in at the end of the last game, and it carried on. Sticks were guns, a copse of trees the jail, the goalposts the hospital and the field was where the action played out. We played the game and I was jailed.

"Pretend you're as stiff and dead as Rosemary's cat," shouted a senior. "Rosemary's cat, Rosemary's cat, was alive and now it's flat."

All the boys laughed and fell down and stiff horseshoes dotted the grass.

"Rosemary's cat, Rosemary's cat, was alive and now it's flat," chortled the boys down on the field, "Rosemary's cat, Rosemary's cat, was alive and now it's flat!"

The bell rang and they groaned and moved toward the classes.

Handwriting, grammar, reading aloud from the textbook, spelling. The sun moved higher in the sky. The lunchtime bell rang out and my stomach rumbled with hunger. I grabbed my jam sandwich wrapped in paper and sat on the benches with the other boys. The jam had gone through the bread and onto the paper and I licked the paper first.

"Rosemary's cat, Rosemary's cat, was alive and now it's flat," murmured Harold as he looked over at Rosemary sitting with the other juniors. She was eating a cheese sandwich, nibbling at the edges.

He smirked. "I don't think she knows. Maybe we should sing her a little song, boys?"

They laughed and moved their bottoms along the bench edging closer to the juniors. The chant started as a whisper and gradually got louder. Rosemary looked over and stopped eating. Her face collapsed, her shoulders hunched, and the rags in her hair trembled.

I stood up. "Hey, cut it out. She doesn't know . . . She . . . she . . . she's a junior," I stammered.

"Go and cuddle her then, Albie, girl. Go and cuddle your new little girlfriend." The boys ran off towards the field still chanting, with the words still reaching the benches. I stood undecided. I was not on the field, not in the game.

"I found your cat dead. I told Miss Sullivan." My eyes darted to the field and back to the shaking rags. "Mr McIntosh brought it to your house. A car hit it."

Rosemary's head stayed down. I felt my face redden. I saw a small splash of wet fall on her knee. I pulled my balled-up hanky out of my pocket.

"Do you want to use my hanky?"

Rosemary stood up. She faced me and pushed my hand away hard. Her eyes and cheeks were wet. She jutted her chin and nose in the air. She kicked me hard in the shin with her pointy polished shoe.

I turned and ran for the field.

Henrica Schieving *is a teacher who lives in Dunedin. She is a member of the Dunedin Writer's Group. Her writing delves mainly into the perspectives of children and memoir.*

Oh Dear

Clare Marcie

There's a tree here that looks like it's covered in monarch butterflies – from afar.
Up close though, it's these exploding orange-red flowers.
Monarchs have been following me around since I returned home.
I had somehow forgotten about them.
At first, I thought they were pointing me in the direction of a particular person (especially
when he had to dress up as one for a job) but they've remained in my life after he left.
I cannot decide what they are trying to communicate, of course, knowing deep down that I'm
looking to create a sign out of them. I'm forever making meaning.
In Glasgow, it was foxes – they always seemed to carry so much metaphorical weight.
Google indicates that butterflies are a symbol of transformation, change, the
glory of life, mortality.
Sometimes they just give me encouragement, especially when there's more than one and they
flicker and dance together and apart in the sunlight.
The tree that looks covered in them – which I spotted in springtime – fascinates me.
It's like a cherry blossom tree, laden with colour but holding no leaves, only bright exploding
flowers on a tree skeleton.
It's contemporary art.

No foliage to complicate things.
I had forgotten about magnolias too, their blooming a strange surprise – alien to my greyed
city eyes.

Now they're almost done, some splaying open and pink like Play-Doh fireworks, others
swollen ample white like marshmallows bloated in hot chocolate, shedding in chunks to the
earth, bloomed and bruised.
Almost too abundant, they induce blushing cheeks in me
Their unapologetic ripeness is like the space between my legs
Swollen, soft, pink

It's nature's shifts into growth that cannot help but make me think of my own.

Not long ago, I felt my grandmother's cold, soft, leathery skin as I helped to dress her in the Auckland winter – a few days dead.
The confronting simplicity of her aged body in all its imperfection and gathered experience
stilled me.
The moment I knew for sure she was dead was not the coldness of her body but the putting
on of shoes and socks without her knee-jerk ticklish giggle in response.

"Oh dear" she would say when conversation fell into silence.
"Oh dear"

Spring, like any change, is not easy. It's heat and cold, ups and downs as we emerge out of the
darkness blinking bleary eyed.
We stumble like newborns into the new season, no grace but

innocence, openness.
Grandma, as she aged, stayed true to her simple habits. Hash browns with mayo for dinner, handwritten budgets, Catholic trinkets.
I saw her fear of change – though she never articulated it to me.

I'm relearning how to be in this Aotearoa nature, this wildness, learning to love all its parts,
its rhythms and curves, bruises and blossoms alike. There is a pain in change but also a
beauty, an opportunity for freshness.

To begin again.
Salt water and sunshine. The holy heat of lavender and rosemary.
Monarch butterflies are the colours of tigers – fierce and regal, light and gentle, flying
candles that seem to point to something deeper.
They confront me with mortality, with survivor's guilt, with beauty that is not painted on or
Conscious.

Oh dear

When I say that I feel broken and you look away, you are hearing me all wrong.
It is a splitting of skin, a shedding of dead leaves, a wringing out of the old ways.
To go from caterpillar to butterfly is not easy. It is not a violence humans experience – to
cocoon and split skin after skin, to change colour and structure like that – from solid to liquid to solid again.
There is a spiritual symbolism to this process that I take my lessons from now.
To give into the change, to struggle through it, to trust that it is necessary, to allow it to take over.

"Oh dear," grandma would say to all this

Oh dear

Oh dear

Oh   dear

Originally from Nelson, *Clare Marcie is an actor, writer, audio describer and theatre creative based in Auckland. She holds a Masters in Classical & Contemporary Text from The Royal Conservatoire of Scotland in Glasgow. Clare's writing has previously been published in a collection titled Letter to an Unknown Soldier as part of the 1418 Now WW1 Centenary (2014), and you can find out more about Clare's work at her website claremarcie.com*

A Winter Journey

Lorraine Marson

The phone calls – so many phone calls – they were like clarion calls across the miles, over the water and upland valleys, and into the beating heart of the house. Susan flung the tea towel onto the bench. Her outward breath would have barked if it could. Why does June always do this when a meal is about to be put on the table? She kept her busyness to herself, and turned the saucepans with their chattering lids down to low.

She heard Jimmy say, "Hello Junebug, how are you?" his voice fond and cajoling. The lilting tones elevated the mundane words to an urgent enquiry as if he had been waiting for her call all day. How exasperating! Susan thought. She was prone to impatience at the best of times and listening made her heart lurch, as he would never use that tone of voice with her. She tried to think of all the reasons why she was truly grateful that he didn't but, just occasionally, she felt she would have liked to be indulged too.

Susan sat down on the rickety old Regency chair by the window and flipped idly through the newspaper. The thwack of the pages being turned would have been maddening to anyone within earshot, she mused. Unable to concentrate, she put the paper down and sat staring at the reality of Jimmy's Aunt June, hurtling around everyone she knew like so much space dust. She was constantly in touch with family and friends, sharing gossip, appropriating little stories to circulate with unrestrained mirth. Pity the poor child who couldn't count or whose lumpen limbs wouldn't carry them across the finish line. No-one was safe, especially not their child, Ella, who, when young, was plump and naughty and never wanted to please.

June had risen in the diplomatic service at a time when women just didn't, and had an imperious air that comes from bossing other people around, coupled with a total conviction in her own opinions. She was in her seventies now, still formidable. Susan's smile didn't reach her eyes as she remembered part of a conversation the last time she had seen June:

"Who was that Canadian chap, mad name, born in Ceylon, wrote that book about India, God! Rajasthan is beautiful at this time of the year! He's got a new one out we must all read."

"Oh," Susan had said, "you mean Ondaatje, Michael Ondaatje."

"That's the fellow."

"It's Sri Lanka now, June," Susan had said. She of all people should have known that. "And it was set in Italy . . . but there was a character who was an Indian sapper. . ."

"Never mind," June had said in dismissal, her head already turning to interrogate her next victim.

She never listens. Susan could hear Jimmy enquire about her day, his tone solicitous, but preoccupied. Their conversations were like static coded bursts of fire crackling down the line. Neither one really listened to the other. "Good, good, see you then old girl," she heard Jimmy say. How he got away with that she would never know, this curious relationship between nephew and spinster aunt reaching back to when he was a small boy.

"June's coming to visit, just a few days, staying with Beverley this time," Jimmy said, when he came downstairs.

"That's nice. Shall we have a dinner for her? Which night would suit?" She found it easier to pre-empt the inevitable, her own busy life as head of department at a local high school a mere trifle. Her job tired her, often bored her, her days spent in endless administration but her career was never alluded to and she was partly to blame. She couldn't trust anyone in Jimmy's family with her unguarded thoughts and opinions.

"Yes, I already suggested that. She thinks the Friday, as Saturday they they're going to the concert and then out to dinner."

The taxi drew up at five o'clock. Susan had tried to tell June dinner wouldn't be until eight, but knew June would always make a point of adhering to her own archaic time lines. Peering out from behind a curtain in an upstairs bedroom, Susan could see the furious activity that always heralded June's arrival. A box was ceremoniously carried aloft by the taxi driver and, parting the curtain a little further, Susan witnessed June directing proceedings. June's hunched back as she bent over her parcels was draped in a beautiful shawl that had dropped to the ground off one shoulder. Beverley, her arms full, bent down to pick it up and June –though Susan could hardly bear to watch – turned and the shawl twisted around her arm as if Beverley had meant it to and sent June's parcels sprawling. Now she could see Jimmy, who would pay the taxi driver and pick up the parcels, his soothing words amid all the activity acting like cushions as they billowed into the house. Susan quickly applied her lipstick and stood erect. She had spiked up her hair for a different look but knew it would be met with silent disapproval. She rushed down the stairs so as to be ready.

Here were the presents, each more inappropriate than the one before. June would insist on buying Susan clothes and Susan, unwrapping the parcel now with sinking heart, knew there was an unspoken insinuation that she didn't know how to dress. It was a silvery grey cotton blouse with puffed sleeves that tapered away at the wrist. Oh God, there was absolutely nothing to be said, thought Susan, as she piled one thank you on top of another. June, as always, was so pleased with her purchases it didn't matter how they were received, she was at her indefatigable best in the bustle of giving.

"Oh, this colour looks adorable on you," she said, holding the wretched thing up to Susan's face. "Look how it brings out your eyes."

Her own were framed in thick black eyeliner flicked up at the sides, her hair a rigid bouffant decades old. "You need to find out what suits you Susan and just stick with it," June had said to her once.

Now she remarked on Susan's pale complexion, "A little blusher dear, you should always wear it."

Susan averted her eyes and looked down at the daft array of expensive frippery she would discard at the first opportunity. The burden of receiving was never to be underestimated; she felt a flush start at her neck under its suffocating weight. Thank goodness they had moved cities. Her onslaughts, while more intense, were fleeting. June was like a giant wave that sucked the life out of you and left you gasping on the beach. Jimmy bobbed up ready for the next one but Susan didn't have the knack. She didn't know the rules and never would.

Beverley, just back from a conference in Australia, gave Susan a look that was conspiratorial in its kindness. Though Beverley was a few years younger than June,the two women had known each other since they were girls at boarding school. Beverley had written two successful biographies of important political figures and had become well-known later in life for her poetry as well. She was wry and funny and her keen intelligence always seduced Susan, who would look for an opportunity somewhere in the evening to talk to her alone. It could be on the most mundane of subjects but Beverley's wit and insight always elevated the conversation to another level.

Jimmy was now in courtly attendance to both June and Beverley. Susan could sense his pride in his aunt, oblivious to the exasperation that she often felt. He appeared to expect her acquiescence and, through bitter experience, she found she preferred to remain silent and let plans be made for them whenever June was around. It was easier that way. "The sweetest of women," she could hear June say regarding her passivity. She let that go too as she stood outside Jimmy's family because she was constantly told she was a cherished part of it.

Susan watched June now with trepidation. Her face was animated and slightly flushed, the heavy make-up starting to shine, as she sailed through the funk of her great niece's presence with no hesitation whatsoever.

"What do you mean dear? Fashion! Those shorts are very short and your stockings . . . they're laddered."

"They're tights," Susan could see her daughter mouth under her breath.

"What dear? But under shorts!"

June had given Ella an Alice band jewelled with agate and topaz. Ella sneered in disgust but June didn't notice.

"How well it suits you dear – keeps all that hair from your face. You know, she's quite pretty, Susan, when she tries."

How could she get it so disastrously wrong? thought Susan, embarrassed by her daughter's silent scorn. The knowledge that Jimmy wouldn't understand the nuance in a hairband, and that another unpleasant scene between father and daughter would ensue later, didn't help either.

Susan had to admit though, in the course of the evening, that June's visits left no lasting harm as there would be no reproach, no matter who was badly behaved, as June simply wouldn't notice. There was no evidence either that there would be any obligation in the years to come which also helped to engender a slight softening toward her.

Suddenly June was on her feet, "Come, Bev, we must march on. Jimmy will take us home won't you darling?"

Susan slowly finished the rest of the tidy-up, her daughter having slipped unseen back to her room even before the house had emptied. The sitting room was still in candlelight and she decided to play Schubert's *Winterreise*; an indulgence as she was alone, her own piano playing now a memory. The melancholy music and the candlelight that flickered and lit the dark recesses of the room, seemed to light those thoughts she always tried to keep hidden. These endless family obligations overwhelmed her sometimes and left her numb and alone. She would continue to be loved.

Tucking her feet up under her in her favourite chair she listened with deep concentration to the music. After a time, she could see the trees outside swaying and knew there would be a storm. Perhaps Jimmy would be caught on the bridge, he and the car sliding chaotically across the slipway, crashing then dropping down into the harbour, his mutilated body unable to swim for safety and his face becoming less and less distinct the way a loved one's face does in the shock of death. Gone in an instant her secure but faltering union; gone too, the constant noise of the family and the endless negotiating. She was tired of performing, tired of Jimmy's blind adherence to family. Suddenly appalled at where her unchecked thoughts had led her, she got up and poured herself another glass of wine. Perhaps it was the deep pathos in the music. The song cycle was nearly at an end and she felt a sense of release in this haunting music, as if she could almost bear the loss and still continue to live her life.

"Turn that shit off, Mum, I'm trying to do my homework," Ella shouted down the stairwell. Susan knew her less than studious daughter would have only then taken out her headphones as she shuffled between iTunes, Facebook and YouTube. However, she turned the music down and, as the piano faded, and that beautiful voice ebbed away, she heard the humming of an engine in the driveway. She washed, dried and put her wine glass in the cupboard as if Jimmy might catch her anarchic thoughts in her empty glass.

"Where have you been?" she said, as he walked in the door. "You've been gone for nearly two hours. Beverley's only over the bridge."

"You know June, quite forceful when she wants to be – regaling us with stories from the past. She insisted on a late supper. I couldn't refuse her. It's bitterly cold out there now and blowing like a bitch. Felt a bit precarious on the bridge actually. I'm off to bed."

Yes, she didn't reply, she did know June and knew it pleased him to be so cherished. It was a flaw she would never confront but could only wonder at how June's many friends, formidable in their own right – June would accept no less – could indulge her too. Perhaps the flaw was hers, and hers alone, she thought to herself as she mounted the stairs.

"You need to watch your P's and Q's young lady!" Jimmy's raised voice made her turn back down the stairs again. She could hear the wind wrap itself around the corner of the house and tug at the flashing Jimmy was supposed to have repaired. The rain had started now and she watched as it washed over the huge picture window, great swathes of water sluicing down onto the patio below. She heard the slam of a door above and made her way back up the stairs to the comfort of a long bath behind a locked door.

Beverley and Susan were sitting in an empty café mid-afternoon the following week having met by chance. Susan was pleased at this impromptu encounter, as she only ever saw Beverley in June's company and there was always, though unspoken, a script ordained over time that they would dance around in the first moments of conversation. Beverley was relaxed, her sleek white hair elegantly coiled in a knot at the nape of her neck. Susan looked at her face and was startled in that simple act of really looking to discover Beverley's beauty - an older woman laying claim to a younger woman's dominion. But it was her eyes - lapis lazuli blue - their intensity unfaded by age that were most affecting. She felt diminished in their flawless gaze away from the qualifying influence of June.

The conversation quickly turned to June, as a leveller, and it was hard after they had moved on to other topics for Susan to concentrate. Her eyes still looked into Beverley's but now she could see their colour harden and glow with the untamed release of the words she had spoken. Could there have been an affair, long ago, which had faded, or more likely ended in betrayal, June galloping over Beverley to her next lover? Unthinkable. But it was as if there was an unread text for all to see in her eyes. Susan had often wondered at a rather different sexual orientation than Jimmy's family could ever allow for or even acknowledge existed.

She was aware she appeared to be listening too intently, but Beverley seemed unaffected and told her a very funny story about another writer given easily to hubris, and his humiliation at the hands of a mercenary critic. Susan, though fascinated, as this was a world far removed from her own, kept turning those words about June over in her mind.

"Oh heavens, Susan, I simply cannot stand the woman! I do everything in my power to keep out of her way. We all do!"

It came to her as they parted on the steps outside the café, and she walked into a chill wind on High Street, that there would be a silent obligation with this knowledge too. She wrapped her unbuttoned coat around herself, lowered her head and pressed her nose into its protecting folds.

Lorraine Marson *has written short stories, which have been published in takahē and Headland. A graduate of AUT MCW, she has just completed her first novel, which was longlisted in 2018 for the Michael Gifkins Prize for an unpublished manuscript.*

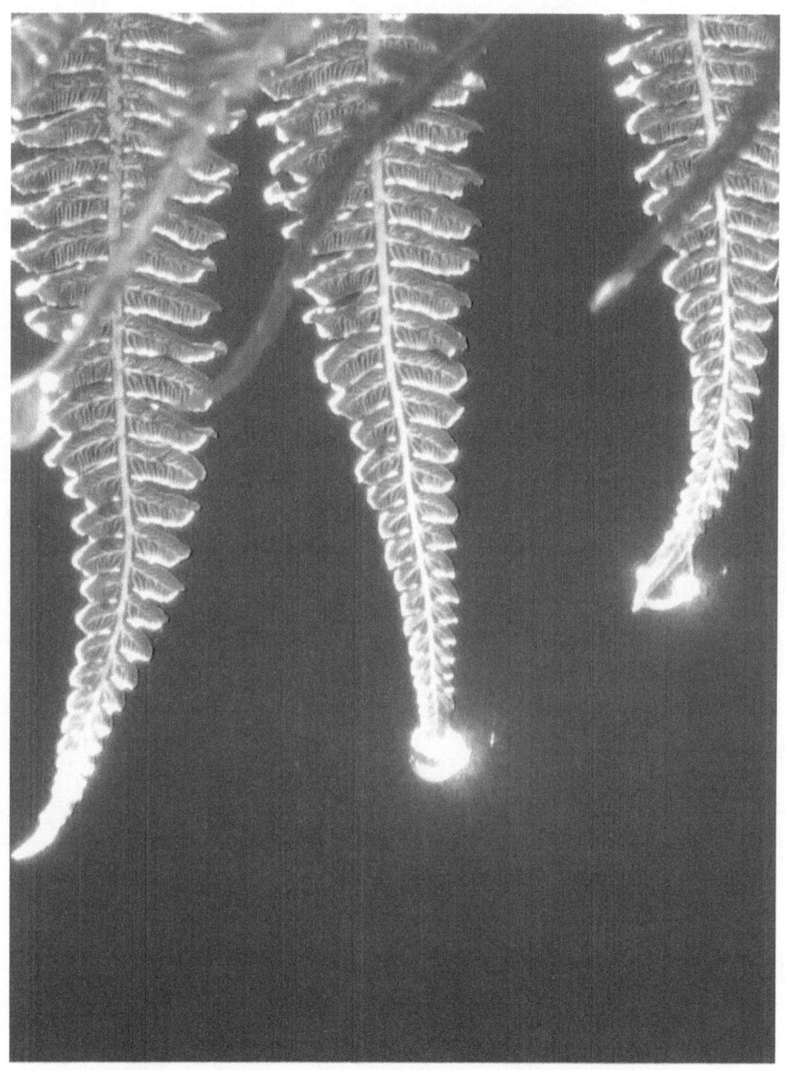

Morning Dew — Photograph by Ellie Stiggers

Ellie Stiggers *is an aspiring photographer. Following completion of her final year at Green Bay High School in Auckland, she intends to study Visual Arts at university in 2020. In the future she would like to travel around Asia and teach art.*

Mama

Lee Tupuola-Madsen

I want to go back
    to when you knew me
Standing
Waiting
Under tree
Salu in hand.

I want to go back
    Eyes Resting
Talking
Laughing
Breathing
    Warmth
Winter frost

Take me back
to the time
    of Falling
Magic butter
Mother curses
    Sequined frocks

I want to go back
    Please take me
Mothball purses
Salu scraping
    The Days of our Lives

Take me back
and Keep me
Frozen.
    In Sadness
not grief
    Rapt,
I'd stay.

Lee Tupuola-Madsen *is a Samoan poet, whose work is heavily influenced by her life, her identity and her family. Her poem Mama is a dedication to her maternal grandmother, Peseta Su'eileololemanumalo Sophia Skelton (nee Hughes) who shaped her life and her heart.*

Renovation

Christina O'Reilly

The builder, whose name was Mike, was fiftyish, weather-beaten and kind. "I see your problem," he said, tapping both sides of the wall with his knuckles. "It does seem to be taking up a lot of room for no good reason. Sounds hollow," he added. "May be an old pantry or something."

In her mind's eye, Rachel could see the new stainless steel kitchen bench spanning the length of the wall to where the French doors opened into the dining room. At the moment, the progress of this dream bench was impeded by a metre-square rectangular protrusion, which reached from the flagstone floor to the ceiling. "I just want it gone," she said.

"There's probably rotten wood behind there," Mike muttered, picking up a crowbar and inserting it into a join in the wall. "That's probably why it's boarded up." He tapped the end of the crowbar with a small hammer and ancient dust fell onto the floor.

Rachel glanced nervously at her watch. He had turned up late and now it was almost four o'clock. Right on cue, the front door slammed. Her heart sank.

A moment later, Jasmine appeared in the kitchen, her long, straight hair hanging limply either side of her spotty face. She glared at Rachel and flung her schoolbag onto the breakfast bar – a movement that briefly raised the hem of her extremely short skirt even higher.

"What do you think you're doing?" she asked in a low but loud voice.

Rachel took a deep breath and composed her face into a smile. "Hi, Jasmine," she said. "I hope you've had a good day."

Jasmine regarded her with loathing. Very slowly she shook her head, as if to say *don't even try to pretend that you care.*

Rachel felt herself blushing and turned away. "I told you. I want to renovate the kitchen and Mike here is going to do it for me. For us," she amended.

Jasmine leaned forward and spread her hands over the old breakfast bar. "You just want to get rid of every trace of Dad. First his clothes – and now this! You're a disgusting, unfeeling bitch."

Mike put his tools down with a clatter. "Now, steady on. . ."

"Mind your own business!" Jasmine snapped. "It's nothing to do with you." Grabbing her schoolbag, she flung herself out of the room, slamming the door behind her.

There was a moment of tense silence. "Sorry," Rachel said, glancing up to catch the look of outrage on Mike's face. "It's okay. She's a teenager. She's taken her father's death very hard."

But as she said this, she couldn't help thinking that all the time that Stuart was really ill – his diagnosis was made just after they had bought this huge, expensive old house – when she, Rachel, could have done with some help, his daughter had basically ignored him or was impatient and nasty with both of them. In the last few weeks before his death, Stuart had sat for hours at that breakfast bar, a bald, vacant stranger, the tumours blooming in his brain slowly squeezing out all the parts of him that made him dear to her.

"In a way, Jasmine's right, of course," she said now. "There are some things I'd really rather forget."

Mike looked at her with an expression that since Stu's death had become so familiar to her: pity mixed with confusion, a not knowing what to say.

In reply, he picked up his tools and said gently, "Shall we take a look at what's behind here then?"

Despite its age, the front piece of board, like a large door without a handle, came away cleanly. Mike lifted it to one side and together they peered into the space behind it. A succession of shallow, very deep shelves, scattered with dust and mouse droppings, stretched from floor to ceiling. "An old pantry. Just as I suspected." Mike took a flashlight out of his tool belt and shone it into the back of the cupboard.

"Hang on a minute." There was a note of surprise in his voice. "Take a look at this." He stood back to let Rachel get closer. In the beam of light she could see the outline of quite a different structure on each of the ascending shelves.

"It's a staircase," she said. Looking up, she saw that the top step now formed part of the pantry ceiling. "But where on earth does it go to?"

The builder raised his eyebrows. "They look like back stairs – for the servants perhaps, back in the day. So, maybe to the first floor and then the attic?"

"But there's no access to the attic from the first floor. Not that I know of anyway."

Mike shrugged. "Shall we take a look?"

Rachel led him out to the hallway and the main staircase. Here, the numbing thud of rap music vibrated heavily in the air.

"Your daughter has an interesting taste in music," Mike remarked as they made their way upwards.

Rachel smiled tightly. "Actually, I'm the wicked stepmother."

He nodded. "Ah."

Half an hour later, they were no wiser – there seemed to be nowhere that a staircase could possibly *go,* even if it had been boarded up behind the walls – and the deafening and repetitive noise emanating from Jasmine's room was fraying Rachel's nerves.

Mike looked at his watch as they went back down to the kitchen. "I'm going to have to go now," he said, levering the heavy board back into place and securing it with a couple of nails. "I've got another job on for the rest of the week, but I'll be back on Monday. In the meantime, have a think about what you want to do. Keep this as a pantry, demolish the stairs that are in there and remove the whole thing, or we can break through the ceiling and investigate where they go to, if anywhere. You decide."

All that evening, as she made a careful lentil stew for Jasmine, who had recently gone from being a lax vegetarian to a strict vegan, and fried a small piece of steak (with all the windows open) for herself, Rachel thought about the hidden staircase. It would be impossible not to make an attempt to find out where it led – and now she had almost a whole week to wait before the builder came back.

"You've been cooking dead flesh again."

Rachel jumped as Jasmine came up behind her. "Must you call it that?" Normally she wouldn't rise to the bait but the girl had caught her off guard.

Jasmine's eyes gleamed with satisfaction as Rachel handed her the bowl of lentils. "I'll take this up to my room. The smell down here is nauseating. And so is your breath, by the way."

Rachel gritted her teeth as rage rose like acid in her throat, but Jasmine just shrugged and added, "All meat eaters' breath stinks."

When she'd gone, Rachel sat down at the breakfast bar and put her head in her trembling hands. Would a daughter of her own have been so unrelentingly horrible, she wondered? She knew teenagers could be difficult, but even when their mothers didn't seem to like them very much there was still love there, unconditional and unwavering. How long was it since she had even spoken to any of those mothers, those friends?

The ghostly image of her own daughter, the longed for one who invaded her dreams and would never be born – endometriosis had put an end to all that – floated before her eyes. She'd be a friend, a soulmate and a confidante.

"We'll always have Jasmine," Stuart had said when Rachel's infertility had been confirmed. It was meant as a comfort, a consolation prize.

The bass beat of music upstairs thudded against her eardrums. Rachel lifted her head and pulled her dinner plate towards her. She cut into the steak, rare and bloody, just how she liked it.

The next morning, up late after a virtually sleepless night filled with guilt and remorse at her own feelings, she caught Jasmine just as she was leaving the house.

"How are the counselling sessions going, Jazz? I hope it's helping."

The girl turned towards her, holding the front door open with one hand. Her face was blank. "I haven't been going," she said. "Not for weeks. Not since I caught him looking up my skirt." She smiled. "Thanks for asking though. And it's Jasmine to you. Only my friends call me Jazz."

Rachel stared at the door as it closed behind her. "So what have you been doing with all that money I've been giving you for the train?" she shouted. Her voice echoed up the empty stairwell.

Years of bottled up rage and frustration gave her a strength she never knew she had. Stu's tools were still in the garden shed; she used the electric drill to remove Mike's nails and the sledgehammer to break up the shelves. Exhilaration pulsed through her veins as the thin wood splintered and fell apart.

An hour later, the steep oak stairs were cleared and exposed in all their shabby glory. The bottom step creaked as Rachel stood on it and heaved the sledgehammer up towards the ceiling. It was too heavy. Sweat dripped down her face, stinging her eyes. Back out in the shed she found a smaller hammer and, eventually, a crowbar. Using Mike's method, she inserted the crowbar between the ceiling and the wall and tapped the end of it with the hammer, finally loosening the far corner enough so that she could get the fingers of both hands behind it. Taking a deep breath, she pulled down with all her might.

The ceiling came away with a sudden crack and hit her hard on the forehead. Rachel fell back against the wall, dazed and panting. Wiping her eyes with the back of her hand, she looked up, into total blackness. She felt for the stairs and began to climb up, but was soon overcome with such an oppressive feeling of claustrophobia it took her breath away.

Rachel's heart thumped as she backed out into the familiar light of the kitchen. Her left hand was covered in blood and still more was dripping onto the debris at her feet. Her forehead began to smart with pain.

In the downstairs bathroom she retrieved a first aid kit from the cupboard and looked up into the mirror. A madwoman, her face covered in blood, with greyish, dusty hair and wild eyes, stared back at her.

The basin filled with bloody water as she sponged her face with a flannel, mopping carefully around the profusely bleeding wound. A sudden wave of nausea and she was on her knees retching into the toilet. Afterwards, holding a cotton pad to her head and feeling slightly better she sat, impatient and shaking, on the edge of the bath for what seemed like hours, until the bleeding finally stopped.

Back in the kitchen with Steri-Strips on her forehead, Rachel filled a large glass with water and drank it straight down. Then she fetched the torch.

This time the claustrophobia was not so bad. She climbed steadily upwards – the stairs were narrow and very steep – until she reached a tiny flat landing. The torchlight around her feet illuminated piles of vermin debris and the remnants of some kind of nest. Rats. She had always wondered about the scuffling noises in the ceiling.

Rachel shuddered and shone the torch upwards. Ahead of her was a single door with a large round handle and a keyhole. It was locked.

"Of course it is," she said out loud into the silence. After all that hard work her exasperation was intense. She shone the torch around the edges of the door without much hope, but then discovered a key hanging from a hook just to the right of the doorframe. It was a stroke of unbelievable luck. Rachel's hand shook with excitement as she inserted it into the keyhole.

After the darkness of the stairs, the sudden flood of light when the door swung open made her squint and raise a hand to her eyes. The room was small, narrow and rectangular with a wide-planked wooden floor and a single iron bedstead wedged in at the far end. A crudely fashioned skylight, spattered with bird droppings and rotting leaves, created a freckled pattern on the walls. There was evidence that it had leaked; one of the floorboards beneath it was spongy underfoot. To her left there was a small window, barred on the inside and almost completely covered with the Virginia creeper that grew rampantly on the outside wall. The room reeked of despair.

It was like a prison cell, Rachel thought: stark and oppressive. By inserting one hand between the narrow bars, she tried to open the window but discovered that it had been fixed to open no more than an inch, just enough to let in some air. She sat on the edge of the thin mattress, sending up little wafts of dust. What had happened up here, she wondered? Who had slept on this hard iron bed?

She must have been sitting there for hours as when she got to her feet her legs were stiff and her back ached. The rest of the day was spent clearing up the mess in the kitchen, cleaning the floor and sweeping the newfound staircase. It was almost four o'clock by the time she sat down at the breakfast bar with coffee and a biscuit; she realised only now that she hadn't eaten all day.

For once she was actually looking forward to Jasmine coming home. This mystery was just what they needed – a research project they could work on together, something to talk and speculate about.

The front door slammed as usual but Jasmine didn't appear. Rachel went out to the hallway and saw her climbing the stairs. With her was a man with a tattooed neck and shaved head wearing tight black jeans.

"Jasmine!"

They both turned towards her and she saw that the man was at least thirty years old. His dark eyes were bloodshot and staring.

Jasmine scowled. "What?"

Rachel bit her lip, determined not to make a scene in front of this menacing stranger. "We talked about this," she said calmly. "You made a promise."

Jasmine raised her eyebrows. "Yeah? Well, I changed my mind."

She grabbed the man by his belt and gestured provocatively towards the bedroom. "Come on, Carl."

Rachel went back to the kitchen, her fingernails digging painfully into her palms. With renewed strength, she manoeuvred the heavy board back into place. The staircase would remain her secret now.

It took five days of painstaking research to discover what she needed to know – the bones of the story. The rest she filled in with her own imagination.

The house had been built by Henry Sullivan, a wealthy wool merchant, in the late 1800s. His wife had died young, of tuberculosis, and he never remarried. He was looked after by a young live-in housekeeper who, in 1895, disappeared in mysterious circumstances. According to the old newspapers, her family suspected foul play but her body was never found. Three years later, Henry Sullivan took in his orphaned two-year-old niece from England, who later inherited the house.

Rachel's research into Sullivan's family revealed that he only had one sibling, a sister who had died in infancy. Where, then, did this mystery niece come from? Rachel wondered as she sat on the hard iron bed. And what had happened to his young housekeeper? Was she the unfortunate soul who had been imprisoned up here? Through the small barred window, the verdant leaves of the creeper rustled in the breeze.

The mystery absorbed all her waking thoughts and she found she barely noticed Jasmine at all. That is, until one morning a few weeks later when she discovered the girl rifling through her handbag.

"What are you looking for?"

Jasmine looked up. Her face was very pale and covered with a light sheen of sweat. "Money," she said.

"Why do you need extra money? Don't I give you enough?"

Jasmine put the bag down. Her eyes flickered with something like fear. "For a doctor. I'm pregnant, if you must know."

She looked so young and vulnerable at that moment that Rachel instinctively put out her arms.

Jasmine took a step backwards. "You don't need to fuss. I'm getting rid of it, and then I'm leaving. I'm going to live with Carl."

Rachel stared at her in silence while a torrent of emotions consumed her body. Then, quite suddenly, everything fell into place.

Rachel smiled. "Don't worry, Jasmine," she said. "Everything is going to be all right."

Rachel filled the kettle and set it to boil on her beautiful new stainless steel bench. It wasn't quite as long as she had wanted but the rest of the refurbished kitchen more than made up for that.

"Have you heard from Jasmine?" Fiona asked.

Rachel turned to her friend with a concerned frown. "No. But then I never expected to. Tough love is just that – really tough."

"Well, I think you did a really good job putting up with her behaviour as long as you did. If she were my daughter, I'd have asked her to leave the minute she was sixteen."

Rachel patted her swelling abdomen. "I hope this one's not going to be nearly as much trouble!"

Fiona smiled. "Sure you don't want to tell me who the father is? You're a dark horse, Rach!"

Rachel smiled and reached for the coffee beans. In the ceiling, a slight scuffling noise could be heard. Rachel grimaced before turning the grinder on.

"Rats," she said ruefully.

But this time it wasn't.

__Christina O'Reilly__ is a writer, freelance proofreader, and copy editor currently living in the Manawatu. Two of her short stories have been published in the anthologies Horizons 3 and The Rangitawa Collection 2017. Her first crime novel, Into the Void, was recently longlisted for the 2019 Michael Gifkins Memorial Prize for an Unpublished Novel.

Dogs of River Road

Tina Shaw

There are a lot of dogs in River Road. If one moves to River Road, there probably ought to be a clause or warning about having to own a dog. The dogs are a varied bunch, like in any small community of individuals, and there's one psychopath.

I've taken to carrying a spray bottle of Exit Mould when I walk my dog Beatrice along River Road. This is to spray in the eyes of a certain white dog called Marley (possibly after Bob) that has attacked our dog on the road, drawing blood and frightening the bejesus out of her. Initially, I took a short iron poker along on my walks, until somebody pointed out that a dog would turn its attacking attention onto me instead if I used a poker on it. We discussed making a chilli spray, and that was still an option. The Exit Mould, after all, might blind a dog. And part of me, although I hate the menacing dog, doesn't want to see an animal blinded. An internet search tells me that yes, this product can cause eye damage. So, I've left the Exit Mould behind and gone back to carrying the iron poker.

My partner walks Beatrice with his walking stick to protect her. This is a gnarly homemade kind of walking stick, around two metres tall, with a steel foot. Perhaps we are overreacting. Certainly, we are being over-protective, as one would with a child who cannot protect themselves from a bully. Even with a minor hurt, Beatrice squeals and freezes like she's just lost a limb. She is now petrified of white dogs.

Beatrice is just eight months old, and already quite large – an English pointer, she will get larger yet, certainly taller, and perhaps develop a bit more chest. Her gait, from the rear, is a kind of jinking cycling motion, like the skinny cyclists who train along Broadlands Road for the annual Ironman event.

On the day of the last Ironman, we were driving along Broadlands Road – the road was closed to general traffic because of the event, but we had a resident's pass – as we had to drive into town to take our old dog to the vet. Monty was debilitated by a "mass" in his chest, which the vet had speculated might be a lymphoma. She had told me on the phone the day before that she expected to see us "either today or tomorrow". Monty had collapsed at 5.00am when trying to go outside. It was now Saturday, and they were open until midday. And so first thing that morning we drove, my partner and I, towards the town and the vet clinic, with our dog sitting in the back, alert enough to look about yet still very unwell. Unwell in a way that you don't come back from. "Look," I said to Bruce, pointing at the triathlete cyclists up ahead, with their lean rumps and long legs making that cycling motion: "That looks just like Beatrice."

Beatrice lies curled like a capital C on our bed. The bed used to be Monty's privilege – snoozing on the "litter bed" in the morning while I had my cup of tea and scrolled through the internet on my laptop – but since he has passed away, we let Beatrice onto the bed now. She gallops down the hallway and leaps enthusiastically onto the bed, landing on my lap, all snout and ears, or threatening to fly off the other side of the bed altogether. She hasn't quite finessed her timing yet.

"Incoming!" warns Bruce.

If I hear the galloping in time, I can put my cup of tea out of the way.

Further down River Road, Graham has two wire-haired pointers. They are enormous beasts, black and white, with yes, wiry coats. He was exercising them one day down at the waterhole when I walked Beatrice down there. At first, she was scared of the beasts, but soon overcame her fear and was running after them like a little kid running after the bigger kids. Graham threw the lid of a paint pail like a Frisbee into the water, and both his dogs rushed into the river to retrieve it. Beatrice looked on at this reckless behaviour with something akin to amazement. Dogs could do that? Jump into the water like that? Graham said something like, "She'll soon be in there, too!" The theory, I supposed, was that our water-shy pointer would see how much fun the big dogs were having and leap into the river as well. That didn't happen, but she did tear up and down the grass with them, especially the younger one who is majestically called Thor. The older one is Birch, so named because the dogs in his line are named after woody things. At any rate, I held my breath and stood off beside a tree, so that a) the dogs wouldn't crash into me, and b) I was ready to jump into the river when Thor and Birch inadvertently pushed my young dog into the current. Neither thing happened, and perhaps I was catastrophising. Again, I felt reduced to the role of protective parent.

The young couple across the road have two grey pig dogs. There used to be more of them, kennelled at the rear of their yard, but lately there only seem to be the two. One of them has the free run of their fenced section and rushes barking up to the fence when we walk past. It has a blunt face and determined eyes. Sometimes I see the young woman walking her baby in a stroller and this grey dog on a leash. Often, she is accompanied by her mother who lives at the end of River Road. It's that kind of place. Pig dogs and family. Several people have relatives also living on the road. Young guys go pig hunting and have boxes on the backs of their utes for their pig dogs and carpet on the bonnet (so the dogs can stand on the bonnet while being driven through the forest to find wild pigs). On the weekends, there's the sound of chainsaws and skill saws and mulchers and ride-on mowers and the chopping of wood. Also, from across the river, the occasional firing of shotguns. Babies in strollers are pushed along the road because there's no pavement.

After a year, we're probably fitting right in, even if in a slanty kind of way: our cousin has bought a house in the street, so now we have family here, and she pushes her elderly terrier along the road in a pushchair – as close as we'll get to babies. We don't have pig dogs, though we do have a chainsaw. So does our cousin.

The young woman, Georgia, got bitten by one of the grey dogs the other day. We heard a ruckus from the street, a scream, and our cousin took off down the driveway to see what was happening. Incidentally, she must have run off in a hurry because her feet were bare on the gravel. Across the road, Georgia was sitting on the tray of her partner's ute, clutching her leg and making a lot of noise. The two dogs had got into a fight; she had stepped in to separate them and been bitten on her ankle. The partner was also upset. "I'll shoot the dog," he kept saying loudly, "I'll shoot him."

Kerry climbed their fence. I wasn't game to go over there myself, though I admired our cousin's temerity. Later she told me how she'd offered to go and see about the baby, who somebody had put into the cab of the ute, presumably out of the way of the hyped-up dogs, and it was also making a lot of noise. "I had to pick it up," she sniffed, not having had anything to do with babies or toddlers before, "and it slung its arms out." (Probably in the Moro reflex). "They must've thought I knew all about babies," she said. "With my grey hair, I must have looked like a granny." At any rate, she faked it, holding the baby at arm's length while things settled down.

The guy took Georgia into town to the medical clinic. Later, they shot the dog.

Further down the road, behind a rustic lichen-covered slat fence, is a black dog that used to rush at the gate to bark at Monty. It doesn't seem to bother with Beatrice, though I can hear it breathing heavily like a stalker as we go past. A boy on a bike over the summer told me its name is Pango, meaning "to be black" in Māori. (The road is also a place where boys on bikes cruise up and down during the summer holidays as if we are revisiting the '50s.) Their house is a very nicely painted villa; the woman who lives there with her family is a painter-decorator. A neighbour told me this and said the woman might well do “cashies”. I’d like to ask her for a quote to paint our large bedroom, which is yellow and blue, both in strong tones, but have so far not known how to approach the house because of the dog. Another boy, also on a bike, warned me about Pango. “He looks like a good dog,” I offered, because actually the dog didn’t look that bad, behind his rustic fence. But the boy scoffed in disbelief, “Good dog – *Pango*?” he said. “He’ll take your arm off!”

Then there are the mountain dogs just a few doors down that bark their heads off every time I walk Beatrice past their place. You’d think the owners would try to discipline the dogs, or at least tell them to be quiet, yet the house remains silent, even though I can tell they are home. One afternoon as we passed and as the dogs broke into their usual frenzied barking, a shout came from the neighbour opposite (the ones who own Pango): “Shut the fuck up!”

One afternoon Beatrice is rushed by a large, handsome Alsatian as we go down to the swimming hole. His owner, Ross, is very apologetic – “He just wants to play!” – and cuddles the cowed Beatrice, cooing, “It’s all right, sorry, dear . . .” They have only recently moved to River Road and have bought June’s house. I’d noticed that the new owners had added an extra bar of timber to the front fence, though hadn’t thought that it meant a new dog in the road. “He’s normally good with female dogs,” said Ross. “No harm done,” I said, introducing myself and shaking his hand, internally thinking, *Yet another dog to protect Beatrice from on River Road.*

There hadn’t been this issue with Monty. When we first adopted him from the SPCA he had been very submissive and lacking in confidence, but that had changed over the years so that he had become quite full of himself and more than willing to tackle any kind of dog on the street – no matter how large. Great Dane? No worries! He wouldn’t have put up with a young Alsatian rushing him. It would have been an all-out brawl, with Monty doing the brawling. It would have been me saying something like, *So sorry, he doesn’t usually beat up dogs larger than himself!*

People were very kind after Monty's passing. I even got a little homemade card styled as if from my friend's dog, and a potted rosemary plant for remembrance. An email message said, *Thinking of you guys. I am sorry to hear about the passing of Monty – I guess it's going to take some time. Sending some hugs to you and Bruce.*

It's obviously nothing like the passing of a child, and yet . . . And yet, I feel there may be echoes, similarities. Monty was with us for twelve and a half years, and was a constant companion in our household. There's a reason people call their dog "fur child", even if they use a self-ironic tone. We often knew what he wanted, and in various ways he could convey to us his needs and desires. Mostly they revolved around food and walks. Yet there were also times when he just wanted to be near us, to lie on the litter bed (that is, our bed) and roll his eyes back at one of us as if to say, *This is great, guys, the pack's all together on the litter bed!*

Monty died quickly that day, slipping forward onto Bruce's leg as we sat on the floor of the clinic room with him, as if he was resting once again on his human's lap. So fitting, as when Monty was a younger dog, Bruce would get him up onto his lap. Now, Monty looked to be merely asleep. I stroked his soft black ears, thinking he would "wake up" at any minute, not believing he was gone. Eventually we had to go, but it was hard to leave him there by himself – and I was taken back to my mother's death only a few months before, and my difficulty in walking away from her, a part of me unable to accept the reality that she had gone.

Taking Monty to the vet clinic that morning to be put to sleep was one of the hardest things I've done in my life. When people said how sorry they were to hear about Monty, there was a blank where I didn't know what to say.

When I rushed into the clinic that morning, dog and man waiting in the car while I checked if they were open for business, Rebecca the vet asked simply: "Is it time?"

As we drove home that day, over the bridge at Wairakei and through a roil of thermal steam – as if out of one netherworld and into another – it felt as if we were travelling inside a time bubble and that when we finally reached our destination, nothing would have remained the same.

We were stopped at a rural "T" intersection on the way back, to allow cyclists to pass. The Ironman competition was still ongoing, the cyclists peddling like hell along the uneven asphalt, cycling into the future.

And so we journeyed home, back to River Road, back to Beatrice.

***Tina Shaw** is the author of numerous works for children, teens, and adults. Her latest publication is Ursa (Walker Books).*

Savasana (shah-VAHS-uh-nuh)

Kirsty Powell

Morning run, swum, nicely salted, seaweeded and yoga-ed out
on a seagrass floor
Savasana
I lie full length and farewell the young American
who has brought me to this place
Namaste
The yoga app plays on. Gentle music, an interlude, never intrudes,
white noise to safely ignore
Ka pai
First sun creeps over Hikurangi and through my pōhutukawa,
  warming
my toes and the ceiling
Revealing
Not the fly dirt or blood-squashed mosquitoes, nor the state
of the paint, nor the worst of the nation
Peeling
Past a blowing curtain and a cheap glass trinket that sends
a thousand rainbows across my ceiling

Believing
Beyond a wars of words, Twittered across a universe
sinking under plastic falsehoods
Terrifying
To think once the music is done my hand will reach
to connect and hear the latest Trumpet
Burnt crumpet
Small offerings to unsettle even me, lying here safe on my shaky island
a whole Pacific away
shah-VAHS-uh-nuh
Google, the bringer of truth, provides the definition
Savasana – corpse pose, even here, even now.
Namaste

Kirsty Powell *grew up in a rural landscape east of Eketahuna. She enjoys writing strong New Zealand characters into her short stories and poems. Her debut novel, The Strength of Eggshells, is due for release by Cloud Ink in 2019. It is contemporary fiction with a part-historical post-war setting in the remote Mangapurua Valley beyond the Bridge to Nowhere.*

Sarong

M.A. Wilkins

A body lies on a king-sized bed, on top of the duvet, but covered by a thin, cotton sarong. Surely the person who created this garment didn't design it for the use of a flimsy blanket, but that's what it has become.

In places, the fabric has faded from hours spent under the sun combined with the bleaching effect of sea salt. The swirls of blue and green intermingle, creating an almost tie-dye effect. I only have to look at the sarong to think of white sand, granules so tiny and soft that it feels like flour under my feet.

The fabric rises a little as the body breathes in, a rasping wet rattle that sounds like mucus stuck in the lungs and throat. Or it sounds like drowning. Pink cauliflower lungs filling up with salty water that doesn't belong there. Maybe the sarong ended up exactly where it was supposed to, by the water. After all, our bodies contain mostly fluid.

It's another minute before the body breathes again. Each time the chest rises I think it will be the last inhalation. This has been going on for hours and there's a part of me that is wishing for the final one and another part that is dreading when it comes, because I don't know which will be the last until after it has passed.

You can go now, I think. You don't need to be in any more pain.

I can't say this out loud because there are ten other people in the room.

I'm holding the hand; it's still warm, but only from the heat of my own skin. I slide the tips of my fingers to her forearm. It is cold.

There are intermittent sniffles from the others. I stay silent.

Another rasping rattle breaks the stillness, then quiet. I hold my own breath; I'll wait to breathe until she does.

My lungs betray me and suck in fresh oxygen before I hear a rattle signifying my release.

I fix my eyes on the weathered sarong, trying to focus on how I remember it floating around this body when it was more alive. In one part of my mind I can see the waves breaking on the sand, the sarong damp from being held against drying togs. But back then the sarong was brighter – the hue heightened compared to today.

The other part of my mind stays in this room, just waiting for the rattle. That can't have been the last one. I lean in closer, listening for some semblance of an inhalation. I'd settle for even just a gurgle of the lungs moving, working.

Silence.

M.A. Wilkins *is a writer based in Auckland. She completed her Master of Creative Writing at AUT in 2017 with First Class Honours and the Dean's Award. Mary is currently doing her PhD in Creative Writing at AUT. She uses her writing as a platform through which to discuss mental health, predominantly in the young adult genre.*

Forty-Three Years of Sunrises

Lisa Williams

Mata's nephews, Tama and Toa, carry 43 years of sunrises down the steps. An irony: a tattoo of Te Rā flows around Toa's biceps. A silky marriage of ink and flesh that begs caressing. Though not by me, an old woman dismissed in the quick flick of his eyes.

They set the card catalogue cabinet in the sand. Oak with solid brass drawer handles, it is one of 100 sold off as surplus to requirements by the Austrian National Library 20 years ago. The 16,000 cards it contains will take all night to burn, though this end of the beach will attract few gawkers. The late dog walkers are a pensive breed, their animals an excuse to air their thoughts to the night sky. Those who venture this far won't approach, leaving Mata and me to get on with it undisturbed.

In exchange for her help, Mata demands a story. She's convinced there's a life crammed into the cabinet's drawers – an eccentric's memoir filed chronologically by year. Just such a tale once appeared in the British tabloids: "Cloth Covers not Good Enough for Daft Dame of Deutschland's Diary". I was back in London doing *Sweeney Todd*, an extended run, so I brought the card catalogue with me. Somehow, they heard about it and mangled the story, of course. About what the cards meant, about me being German.

Not that Mata would have known anything about that. New Zealand turned its back on me 50 years ago when I dropped out of London's Royal Academy to go sing in the ugly tongue of the bloody

"Narzis".

No, Mata wouldn't believe that of the two of us, hers has been the more meaningful life. She lives in the house she was born in and runs the dairy she inherited from her mother.

"This was a bloody good year." She hooks her finger through the handle of the drawer labelled 1977. "Disco? Bee Gees? You probably partied with the lads, eh?"

I chuckle. Mata's misconceptions about my career are legion.

"Musical theatre actresses are *workhorses*, darling. We had no time for partying."

Incredulity turns her brown eyes into saucers. "Would have made an exception for Mr Barry Gibb."

The fire snaps and pops, voicing impatience for its promised titbits. The main meal is a wheelbarrow full of wood deposited behind our sand chairs. Mata has built up a healthy blaze. Unchecked, she'd unleash a bonfire.

"The cards are a record. My scribblings each day about the sunrise. Here, give me one . . . a handful. From anywhere."

She chooses June 1990.

"That'll do." I squint to read the cards. Although it's 8.00pm, I can see just well enough to decipher my faded handwriting. "June 13. Birds fly across it. June 14. Reluctant. Almost sleeping as it comes up. June 15. Voices again. June 16. Warm today. June 17. Sweet. A plum."

I toss the cards into the fire. Mata frowns. "But where *were* you?" she asks.

"1990? We hadn't yet moved back to Vienna . . . so that means Berlin." Only when we were touring, did I bother with place names.

Mata folds her arms across her chest. She has a way of standing like a rugby coach. Useful for intimidating children nicking lollies from the dairy.

"The cards were my lucky charms, that's all."

"A rabbit's foot is a lucky charm, Gillian. This . . . this is OCD!"

"Who are you to know my life?" I snarl, and immediately I'm sorry. Without my husband Paul standing watch, my temper flares.

When I made my travel arrangements to come home, I had intended to stay in New Zealand for only a month. Grief convinced me I could outrun the pain of Paul's death. In Vienna, our friends had formed a silky cocoon around us that kept us safe. After he died, the cocoon collapsed into a shroud that threatened to suffocate me. Here, protected by a half-century barren of memories in the one place I refused to bring him, I imagined I could breathe.

Only the flu I caught in transit kept me from turning right around and flying home. On landing in Auckland time buckled, and I was the 19-year-old girl with the op shop suitcase desperate to board a boat and flee. That I hadn't been in New Zealand for so long meant the unmitigated past could sink its talons into my chest. The child I was couldn't cope with the burden I now bore: losing the love of my life.

En route from Europe, my baggage had gone missing leaving me with only the clothes I'd worn travelling. The bach I rented had no phone and my foreign mobile couldn't connect to the network. The summer holidays had just ended, and the street was deserted, the 'neighbours' returned to the city. Every day at 2.00pm, a dog howled for 20 minutes, plaintive enough that I came to believe it was as abandoned as I.

I spent three days in a lumpy bed with a fever. No groceries, just a bag of cereal, instant coffee and a jar of yeast spread left behind in the pantry. On the morning of day four, I had to decide between a shower or a trip out for supplies. I lacked the stamina for both.

I never learned to drive, so my only option was to walk. The bright sunlight made poached eggs of my eyes. My knees quivered, and with each halting step I battled the urge to lie down on the footpath. A block away, the dairy loomed like a gaudy mirage: bright green with dark green highlights, a brick and mortar advertisement for an energy drink.

One foot in front of the other I pressed on, muddling "I Dreamed a Dream" from *Les Misérables* to keep moving. My brain couldn't stop tangling the words up in two languages: *Ich hab geträumt vor langer Zeit, when hope was high and life worth living. . .*

Mata found me with the sauces staring at a bottle of tomato sauce. It stirred the embers of memory: Jan, my best friend from primary, spelling her name across her chips with tomato sauce.

"You all right there?"

No, I wasn't all right. Rumpled, unwashed, ill. I was *not* all right.

She said I answered in German. She said if I hadn't been wearing such an expensive diamond wedding ring and a dress that cost enough to pay her utilities for a year, she would have rung social services.

The flu left in its wake a profound lassitude. Mata came around every morning with the newspaper and made me tea and toast. She borrowed clothes from a cousin just my size. Such was my fatigue I barely noticed my wardrobe consisted of jandals, track pants and T-shirts. Nor did I take an interest when her niece coloured my grey roots with a brassy red tint a shock rock diva would covet.

Six weeks passed in this way, and to my shame I uttered not a word of thanks. I regarded Mata and her whanau as an unwelcome tether to life. Steely resolve underpinned their kindness. To them, I was the injured bird they would heal regardless of my beastly incomprehension of their good intent. Humour as well as curiosity buoyed their efforts. When Mata discovered I travelled on a New Zealand passport, she couldn't keep the questions from flowing. And which fascinated her more: my answers – scant as they were – or my affected accent?

They mimicked me behind my back and fell about laughing. I didn't mind. They weren't being cruel. The way I talk *is* strange. A German cadence overlaid with a Kiwi inflection, corrupted by my protracted absence.

The first rupture in my depression happened when my baggage, including the card catalogue turned up. Mata treated the suitcases as treasure chests. She draped my dresses, blouses and skirts over the furniture. To "let them air," she said, but really to admire the dance of light across the rich hues and textures. My trousers she strung up like bunting, threading twine through the belt loops. The effect was so ridiculous – *couture* dragooned into service as circus flags – even despair had to give way before it.

Simply passing from the bedroom to the toilet required a meditation on the absurdity of existence. Never had my life been so baldly represented. With its plain, solid history, the bach was the embodiment of memory, the flying pants the identity ego constructs. Put more directly, the bach was my childhood, the pants the life I built once I left New Zealand. The one held up the other. Bulldoze the walls and the clothes fall down.

This knowledge hollowed out a cramped niche I could just fit into that offered occasional relief from grief. It meant I could step away from who I had been and into who I was in the moment. In this place there was no Paul, no guilt. Nothing but the intake of breath and on good days, a walk on the beach.

For this I have Mata to thank. She began dispensing her medicine as soon as she found me delirious in her shop. She bundled me into her ute to go to the doctor. Out of habit, she hit play on the one CD she listens to when driving, and so the Howard Morrison Quartet accompanied us on the way. Because lucidity came and went during that ride, I can't confirm her tale, but she swears she drove off the road when I sang along to *Mori the Hori*, belting out the chorus as if I were on stage.

Although I have found a measure of peace in this quiet town, my voice has forsaken me. I can no longer sing. And this has left me with a loneliness parched as stones baking upon a dry riverbed. Even so, if I wake in the night, I can hear a melody skittering away into the shadows. It's never a piece from the repertoire I built up over my career. It's always a Kiwi number I can't quite place.

The tune is a call beckoning me once more to childhood. This is the tale Mata longs to hear, even though she doesn't know it. People are always drawn to enchantment.

Although there is a danger in telling my story. A fairy tale is an incantation that may conjure evil as well as good. Too late I learned the price. My loved ones have suffered ever since that first morning I rose early to watch the sunrise. It was my 11th birthday, and my present came from the riroriro who gave me the gift of song.

Yet what else besides sharing my story will bring the music back? I cannot resist, no matter the cost. The music has died here, and here it will be resurrected. But I am burning my sunrises to make it clear to the devil who has hounded me through the decades that I understand the debt is mine and no others. An act of provocation and an entreaty. *I will pay this time. At last, I will pay.*

I apologise to Mata for my bad manners.

She replies by pushing out her lower lip. "You're a bloody diva, that's what you are."

"It's not the worst I've been called."

"Too right, it isn't!"

We stare hard at each other, but Mata can't sustain her attempt at a pout. She's too good-natured. "All right then," she says, "we better make a start on these cards."

She glances at the clouds ambling toward the moon. Anaemic looking, but she sees in them the potential for rain.

"Leave it." I gesture toward the card catalogue. Hatred wells up inside me for this beast. Maybe I will burn it too.

"What now? You've changed your mind? Unless we empty it, the boys won't be keen to haul this thing back *up* the hill."

"No. You wanted a story." I scoop up a chain of Neptune's necklace lying close by in the sand – the brown seaweed shaped like a string of pearls.

"Kicked that one for touch."

Mata's revenge for my short temper. Fair enough.

"I'll tell you not one story but three."

"Three!"

"The beginning, the middle and the end."

"Of...?"

"My life."

"Nah, got Google for that. Aunty did a search on you. Says you were quite a beauty back in the day. Masses of red hair, waist no thicker than a man's pinky."

My temper threatens again. I snap the seaweed in two. "If you don't want to hear, well. . ."

She drops into the other sand chair and gives my thigh a swat. "Oh, Gillian. You're a serious one, eh? Too right, I'm keen. Since that first day you came into the shop. 'Now there's a roughed-up wee sparrow with a story.' That's just what I thought. Wouldn't have put so much work into you if I hadn't."

For the 1,000th time, Mata is smoothing my ruffled feathers. She leans forward and looks me in the eye. The humour has gone, supplanted by a solemnity that hints she's harbouring a purpose of her own.

"Shall I start you off with *Once upon a time. . .?*"

"Yes . . . no," I answer, because in the pause between the two words I change the order of my telling. I will begin in the middle where it is safest.

Writer and academic ***Lisa Williams*** *is the author of three novels: Drifting at the Bottom of the World (2003), Death on a Long Winter's Night (2012), and Grandzilla (2018). Grandzilla was shortlisted in the inaugural NZ Booklovers Awards for Best Adult Fiction Book.*

Cormorant in Marlborough Sound
— Woodcut by Manu Berry

Wendy Clarke *is a creative writing teacher who has lived most of her life in Arrowtown. She writes educational resources for teachers, short stories, and she has recently published a children's picture book. Wendy especially likes to write poetry for adults and children.*

Pumpkin Love

Wendy Clarke

When I first loved you,
I planted pumpkins
in dizzy drills,
into a mound of fallow soil.
And without much more attention
than a wash of rain
and a look over from a strengthening sun,
the pumpkins grew.
New leaves intertwined and tumbled
off the mound
and tendrils looped through.
Pumpkins like an emperor's fat pillows
sat roundly on an unmade bed of green.

So singing, 'Love is in the air',
I got out my cleaver
and chopped and cooked and mashed.
We had pumpkin soup, pumpkin scones, pumpkin jam,
pumpkin pies and more pumpkin soup,
staining our mouths and the sheets.
Next spring, I sharpened my spade
and turned over the mound in neat bites.
I combed the soil like thick hair.
It smelt as sweet as crumbled cake.

Fresh Ink

I planted pumpkins in measured rows
and tended each seed as if it were a child.
But they germinated slowly.
The foliage, when it came
was sulky, the shoots stringy.
As summer climbed,
the pumpkins grew,
but they were misshapen and grey-green
like an old man's face.

The night a rogue frost hit my pumpkins,
you said you didn't care
if you never ate pumpkin scones, pumpkin jam, pumpkin pie
and especially pumpkin soup ever again.
I took my paring knife,
the one I use for digging out
the eyes of pocked potatoes
and I stabbed and slashed those ailing plants.
Then wearing my steel tipped gumboots,
I kicked those pumpkins into a field of dock.

Next spring, I saw
the soil was good,
thinner but still vigorous.
So I planted zucchinis.
And as the yolk-yellow flowers
uncurled their skirts
and flashed their stigmata
at the early summer sun,
I put on lipstick
the colour of a damson plum
and went to town.

Dig This

J.A. Grierson

Day 366, navy car park archaeological dig

I've submitted the official report, the one that tells you exactly what I dug up, day by day, for the year that I excavated under the navy museum car park in Torpedo Bay. In land reclaimed by sailors, who cut the cliff and tipped it into the sea, all I found was rubble and sand. Officially.

Now, here's what my report didn't say.

Day 352

My story starts two weeks ago. I was packing up my trowels, shovels and scoops when along came John.

Six foot two and rising fifty, John is Māori. When he was a boy he played home-town rugby and there was talk that he'd be an All Black one day. Now the only traces of a rugby career are the beer gut hanging over the belt of his shorts and an elastic bandage wrapped around one knee.

John shakes the earth, packing down the foundations for the carpark with a machine called "the compactor." He wears ear-muffs but for the rest of us the thuddering is torture.

A man of few words, in the year I've worked here, John spared none of them for me until what was meant to be the last day of our dig. Pallid morning sunlight was creeping over the volcano that shadows our site when the compactor shuddered into unscheduled silence. I looked up. John dismounted, hitched up his shorts, and with lop-sided strides lumbered to the edge of my pit. "Don't pack up your tools just yet, Miss."

I squinted at his silhouette. "We finish the dig today."

"I had a dream last night. You're going to find something – something significant."

"I don't think so, John. We haven't found anything yet and there's only one square metre left."

"You will."

"Do you often have dreams like this?"

"Nope."

"What will we find then?"

"Dunno, but you must keep digging."

John stomped back to the compactor, flicked the ignition and hammered the earth. With a shrug of my shoulders, I picked up my hand shovel, expecting to uncover more of the nothing I'd dug up in the preceding 365 days. But less than half an hour later the metal tip grazed a long, white bone. Pausing to take photographs, with a trembling hand I brushed off the sand and revealed a leg bone. It was thicker than a human femur and terminated in three clawed talons and a horny heel fit for a dragon.

Only one species of bird has ever walked the earth with feet that big and it's been extinct for nigh 1,000 years – Dinornis novaezealandiae – a wingless giant that stood up to 12 feet tall. Within 50 years of Polynesian settlement of Aotearoa – New Zealand – it had become extinct.

There was little doubt how this particular specimen had met its death for its bones were encased in the remains of an ancient Māori oven. Legend had it that the first migratory canoes made landfall in this far-off outreach of the planet here, in Torpedo Bay, but no one could prove it.

I'd barely uncovered the bones when a woman appeared above my pit. She lived 50 yards down the road and I'd seen her coming and going but in the year we'd been neighbours she'd never said hello.

"The energy's changed," she said, pulling up two yards short of the edge, "I felt it from my house. What's happened?"

I pride myself on being a scientist but, looking up at her from the floor of the crater I'd dug, I could have sworn she stood ten feet tall. "How can you sense that the energy's changed from 50 yards away?"

My question sounded ridiculous but the neighbour was staring into the trench as if it was a wormhole that would swallow her whole if she came any nearer.

I looked around my diggings in search of what inspired her dread but all I saw was the usual crumbly mixture of sand, silt and shell, a few lumps of rock, and my moa bones.

"What's that?" she asked.

"We've unearthed an ancient oven with giant moa bones inside it. It could identify this site as the landing place of the legendary Tainui canoe."

She looked impressed. "What will you do next?"

"Send the moa bones off for carbon dating."

With a crease between her brows, she peered round the perimeter of my hole. "You've opened something up. It's powerful. Evil."

I'm a scientist and rely on rational analysis, but the hairs on my arms stood on end. "I'll finish the dig then see what the Ministry of Defence has to say about turning it into an exhibition."

"You won't leave the hole open?"

"That's not up to me to decide."

Her face paled. "I'll come back later, with a friend."

As soon as she'd stalked off, John rematerialised. "Who was that?"

I shrugged. "Someone who says the energy's changed, whatever that might mean."

John scratched the back of his sunburnt neck then sat down on a folding deck chair, not too close to the edge of my pit. "She a witch?"

"There's no such thing."

He rolled a cigarette, lit it and exhaled. "What d'you think she meant, the energy's changed?"

"No idea, but she didn't look happy about it, as if we've opened up a cesspool that'll contaminate her street."

John smoked silently while I went back to my digging. He took his full ten-minute tea-break then flicked the butt from his fingers and ground it under his workman's boot. The sun was gathering heat now, but he stood up and shivered. "You'd better call a tohunga, Mary."

Until then he'd never used my name and I was surprised he knew it. "Why's that?"

John raised grisly eyebrows, and my hackles rose. I'm pure Pākehā – a "pale face" – by definition, culturally insensitive. When we reach the Māori verses of the national anthem, I mumble my way through them because when I was at school we learnt them only in English. Every time I fill out a form asking for my iwi affiliations and I scribble "none" I feel as if I've written "descended from a long line of racist pigs." My ignorance of Māori culture is a handicap but that morning I'd dug up something significant and I wanted some credit for it. Scorn lifted a corner of my lip. "All that's happened here, John, is that we've dug up an oven full of moa bones. The horses of the apocalypse aren't about to ride out from hell. I don't see why we'd need a tohunga."

John shook his head and stood up. I could hear him thinking dumb Pākehā. "Just call a tohunga, Mary."

"What kind of tohunga?" I called up as he turned away. "A tohunga ahurewa or . . . the other sort?" I asked, grasping for Māori vocabulary.

He looked back down at me with an enigmatic smile. Tohunga ahurewa mediate between the atua, or spirits, and Māori gods. They function as priests and I was pretty sure he would suggest one of them.

"A tohunga mākutu."

Now my brows shot up. A long, invisible fingernail ran down my spine. Tohunga mākutu deal with the occult and cast evil spells. A culturally ignorant Pākehā such as myself might translate tohunga mākutu as witch doctor.

I tried to act like a scientist. "I'll talk to our cultural advisers and see what they recommend."

John nodded. "If that makes you feel comfortable, Mary. Or you could do what I say yourself."

"With all due respect, John, you drive the compactor. This site is tapu and warrants a question or two to the cultural adviser."

"Tapu, eh?"

"Yes. I've heard atrocious things happened here, long before the Pākehā arrived, things so terrible that the tapu was never lifted and the village was abandoned forever."

John nodded again. "Makes sense."

Day 353

I'm not superstitious – I'm a scientist – but I felt secretly vindicated when the cultural adviser recommended a tohunga ahurewa – the blessing, not the cursing, kind.

The next day, the neighbour came back. Marching at her side was a short, blonde woman with eyes too young for her face.

"My name is Celeste," said the neighbour, "and this is my friend, Raphael."

Refusing to give the woman the name of an angel, in my head I called her "Blondie".

Blondie frowned into my hole, as if it was fermenting the spawn of hell, then turned to Celeste. "Don't tell me you went in there?"

"No, I stayed back from the edge."

"Thank God for that. It's unspeakably evil."

I, the archaeologist, was standing deep in the unspeakably evil hole, all by myself and wondered if I should be worried by this.

Blondie's glassy eyes roamed around me. "I see bodies, and the severed parts of bodies – fragmented spirits! This was a place of torture and abuse." Blondie covered her eyes and turned away.

I looked around my hole and wondered if I'd suddenly gone blind. I saw no body parts, only the oven, sand, a few pipi shells and broken rocks – and my moa bones.

"Ughhh," said Blondie pulling a bottle of holy water out of her bag and showering as much as she could over me and my hole.

"Would you stop that please? I'm getting wet!"

"Aaah – it's evil, disgusting. We have to clean this out!"

"Stop contaminating my dig!"

"Contaminating? I'm purifying it. You've opened up something ancient and the spirits are ugly. They're laughing at us and saying that they're stronger than God."

"I'm just doing my job," I said, brushing waterdrops from my shoulders.

Blondie threw another dash into the hole, doing her best to avoid me this time, then led Celeste away.

Her performance unsettled me. It hadn't escaped my notice that John had put his director's chair up at a safe distance from the excavations and that no one came within two yards of the edge of my pit. But there I was, in the middle of it.

I'd barely calmed myself down when the commander of the navy base came to talk to me. "Congratulations on your discovery."

"Thank you. I believe it will prove significant."

"Yes, quite. Just thought you'd like to know that we've arranged for a tohunga to perform a ceremony tomorrow."

I stared up at him. He's Pākehā, like me, wearing a crisp white uniform, complete with hat on buzz-cut head. He looked about as culturally sensitive as I did, but he was serious.

"Best if you vacate your dig while the tohunga's here, Mary. Wouldn't want to get in his way."

I fumed in silence for a moment. I didn't like losing control of my discovery, but I acquiesced. "I'll take the morning off."

Day 354

"It's all done," said the commander when I arrived to work. "The spirits have been laid to rest."

Or so he thought.

Day 355

Three days passed before the commander told me, almost

apologetically, "There've been some, er, disturbances in the museum."

"Disturbances?"

"Yes, the ghost of a young boy has been haunting the reception area and museum exhibits have been . . . taking flight."

"Taking flight?"

"You know what I mean."

"No I don't, Commander."

He lowered the brim of his hat and whispered, "Poltergeist."

"I see. Wasn't the tohunga s'posed to sort that kind of thing?"

"We thought he had, but it seems instead he's livened things up. Tomorrow we're having another kind of ceremony."

I raised my eyebrows. He leant closer to me. "Exorcism. With both Catholic and Anglican priests."

I nearly burst out laughing. He saw derision on my face and smiled apologetically. "You can have the morning off again."

Frowning, I nodded. "I'll send the bones off for carbon dating before I go home tonight."

Day 356

High noon, the day of the exorcism, I tried to go to work but patrol cars barricaded the street. Had my site been vandalised? The long face and muted movements of the policeman who leant down to whisper through my open car window looked disproportionately grave. I lowered my car window. "I work here. Is everything alright, officer?"

In the calm, neutral voice that police people are trained to adopt in the face of catastrophe, he said, "There's been a death."

My pulse jumped. "Who died?"

"A father took his five-year-old son for a swim off the wharf this morning but the current sucked the boy under."

"My God!" I gasped, although I'm an atheist.

"Divers are searching for the body. Please turn your vehicle around and leave the scene."

"Of course."

I headed to a café in the village, opted for tea instead of coffee, and ordered a sandwich but didn't touch it. If I hadn't unearthed those moa bones, would any of this have happened? Did the boy-ghost want a playmate, or were the spirits trying to prove that they were stronger than God? My tea went cold.

Late in the day, I drove back to my dig. It was still cordoned off. Frogmen, shaking water from their ears, clustered at the entrance to the wharf. While they stripped off their tanks, men in blue uniforms stretched yellow hazard tape around the scene of the incident.

I parked at a distance and waited till the last of them had left then ducked under the tape. When I stood on the edge of my pit the edge crumbled and I fell into it. In a moment of panic I thought I was going to be sucked under but then I stood up in the bottom and took several calming breaths. I sifted grit through my fingers, searching for something that I can't define. I lost track of time but, as the day grew cold and dark, I told myself that I was being irrational and was just about to scramble out when I saw Celeste approaching.

Without seeing me, she strode onto the wharf. Halfway along, she stopped and stared out to sea then raised both arms heavenwards. For a few minutes, her body stood black against a flaming sky then she lowered her arms and bowed her head for a moment. Turning on her heel, she walked past my pit through the gathering darkness, and left me alone with the spirits on the navy base.

Shivering, I clambered out and walked as fast as I could to my car.

Day 357

When I arrived at work the next day, a short-cropped policeman was pulling down the hazard tape. An ambulance rolled away but the siren was silent.

"You found the body?"

"Yes, first thing this morning."

"Do you mind if I ask where you found it?"

He pointed to the spot on the wharf where Celeste had been standing with her arms over her head. "Searched all day yesterday and found nothing, but the boy was there, gently rocking on the waves, as if he was asleep, this morning."

"Perhaps the body was carried out then washed back in again," I said, but I didn't believe it.

The rest of the day, with trowel, pick and brush, I ransacked my dig. I was on a quest, no longer looking for the remnants of ovens or moas but human remains – anything that would validate what Raphael had said. But I found only sand and rock. Whatever it was – if ever it was – had left no record of its existence.

I'm a scientist but, for once, discovering nothing was a relief.

Day 360

The carbon dating report arrived and confirmed my find – the bones are at least 800 years old. That timing ties them to the first wave of Māori immigration to these shores. I should have been elated but I wasn't. The discovery seemed to have come at too high a cost.

A sailor lowered the white ensign from the flagpole outside the museum, rolled it up then marched off. The museum was closed for the day.

I'd been alone, tidying up, for at least an hour before my stomach rumbled. I stood up and was stretching my back when I caught sight of a Māori warrior – greenstone mere in one hand and feathers in his hair – looming out of the growing dark. I leapt as if I'd touched an electric fence and scrambled out of the pit then a voice rang out, "It's me, John."

My mind cobbled together features obscured by spiralling tattoos. The warrior took a step forward and I sighed with relief at the sight of the elastic bandage wrapped round one knee. "Why're you dressed like that?"

"I'm a tohunga, Miss."

"What kind of tohunga?"

"A tohunga mākutu."

The cursing kind. My stomach shriveled. "What're you doing here?"

"Never you mind. Go home. I prefer to work alone. The others have made the problems worse, but I can handle it."

Now I'm a scientist, not superstitious, but all of a sudden the air around the pit went cold and I heard mocking laughter echoing off the cliffs. "Leave it, John. No one can tackle this alone."

John looked into the pit and his face wrinkled. His eyes rolled back in his head until only the whites showed then he put his hands to his throat and started to choke. Not knowing what else to do, I grappled with his fingers for fully thirty seconds before pulling them off. John's face was ashen and he bent over his knees, panting.

"Let's get out of here," I pleaded. He stood up, breathing hard, and together we staggered off the base to the street.

Day 364

In the daylight, I decided it was all an hallucination and went back to my pit. I wasn't included in the meetings taking place in the museum but the commander did invite me to the ceremony. I declined politely but watched through the wire perimeter fence. A Catholic bishop, complete with crook and flowing robes, his Anglican counterpart, four tohunga and a group of Māori elders wearing feather cloaks stood shoulder to shoulder in front of my pit. The eerie strains of a waiata echoed against the injured cliffs and women wearing piu-piu danced towards the void. John was there with them, as an honoured guest, but he'd washed the spirals from his cheeks and was wearing a suit. Even the Minister of Defence, representing the Crown, attended.

"This must be the most blessed square of car park in the entire world," I whispered to Blondie who was sprinkling her witch's water through the fence. She looked at me and asked, "Has anyone ever told you that you're culturally insensitive?"

Day 365

The day after the ceremony, I packed up at last. The sky looked thunderous and, for the first time in months, rain was forecast. I stretched a thick, black polythene sheet over the pit and battened it down round the edges.

When I'd finished, Celeste turned up. "What've you done? The energy's changed."

"Yesterday there was a ceremony to cleanse and bless the site. Bishops, military, tohunga, politicians – you name it, they held nothing back. Perhaps they laid the spirits to rest."

Celeste tipped her head to one side. "When I came home last night, the energy hadn't changed." She raised an eyebrow then took a step closer to the pit, then another, until, for the first time, she was standing with her toes over the edge. She stared at my black polythene. "You've covered the hole."

"To keep it dry."

"Will they turn your site into a permanent exhibit?"

"No, they'll tarmac it for carparks. The Ministry of Defence put together a budget for preserving it, but it ran to millions. The moa bones and oven have been sent down to Te Papa, in Wellington." Suddenly, I was curious. "You and Blondie – Raphael, I mean – what did you see when you stared into the pit?"

"I saw nothing, but Raphael saw tortured spirits. And you, what did you feel?"

"I felt the sun on my back, grit in my eyes, blisters on my hands. I heard the sound of the sea on the shore, and sometimes I was afraid, but it was irrational."

Celeste nodded.

"What do you do for a job?" I asked.

"I'm a scientist."

I smiled at that. "Not superstitious then?"

"No. I work in nuclear physics up at the university."

"John asked if you were a witch."

She laughed. "Who's John?"

"That's John," I said, pointing to a tall figure strolling towards us with a placard under his arm and a carpenter's belt hanging over the front of his shorts. "He must be putting up a sign to commemorate the moa bone discovery. It almost proves that this was the first landing place of the Tainui canoe."

"That's significant."

Before John reached us, I hurried to ask my fellow scientist, "What do you think really happened? Did we open a wormhole between one era and another?"

Celeste sighed. "I don't invalidate the experiences of my senses just because I don't know how to explain some of them yet. Now you've covered that hole up, the energy's changed back to what it was before. I have no logical explanation for that."

"There are no more spirits who say they're stronger than God? No more demonic laughter?"

Celeste shook her head with a wry smile.

John joined us. "How's you fellas?"

"We're fine, thank you. Does that sign commemorate our discovery?"

John grinned and held it up for us. My face fell as I read out loud, "Navy carpark. Gates close at 5pm."

"Don't worry, Mary," said John, "we know what you found."

__J A Grierson__ read Politics, Philosophy, and Economics at Oxford University and pursued a business career before completing a Master of Creative Writing in 2014. She is a published author of non-fiction and a co-founder of Cloud Ink Press Limited. The first novel in her trilogy, The Last of the Romans, will be published in 2019.

Every Inch

Briana Woolliams

Did you like the colour of my porcelain skin?
See – it took time to delicately craft
Every crease, my parents' making

    They *wove* this

In my mother's womb I was cut from the same cloth
How beautiful it is, to be a part of two
Every stich reflected by imperfectly perfect technique
My mother tirelessly tied every loose stitch

And together, they have worked too hard

    For you to try and undo
    Every inch

***Briana Woolliams** has a Masters of Fine Arts (with First Class Honours). The Tāmaki Makaurau-based maker has a practice that incorporates poetry, sculpture, printmaking, textiles and performance. In 2018, Briana was the recipient of the Todd Trust Scholarship for Fine Art at the University of Auckland.*

Finally, I See

Denise O'Hagan

Faint hands stare up at me from the Formica table. Large windows loom in on the bare cafeteria. A shiver runs down my back. Is it cold or fear? My gaze shifts, takes in this place: bare walls, the air still but for the faint whir of the air-conditioning unit. A whisper might travel a mile in this place.

My fingers fiddle and fidget with nothing. People wander about but don't see me. It's as if I'm not here. The doctor has my number but my phone remains silent. Then I remember I left it at the crash site.

The tea is warm but my hands wrapped around its paper shell feel nothing. Shadows shift behind large panes as darkness envelopes everything outside. Only the rays of light from the street lamps promise hope.

In my mind's eye, I see Josh bent over studying at his desk before dinner, a night out I had said. It could be nice. The befuddled mess of his room a welcome memory now: a half-drunk hot chocolate on the bedside table, clothes strewn on the floor, a pencil marking the page in his history book. My eyes prick with the normality of it all.

* * *

Thai fish cakes with coleslaw for me; David and Josh had steak with fries. Danny Doolans was jam-packed on Saturday night, for the big game on TV. I didn't watch but the boys poured over the screen like tomato sauce.

With dinner over, and half tanked with our usual tipple, we

waltzed up Broadway to the car. Josh gabbled at length about his latest science experiment gone wrong and we all laughed. He jumped in the driver's seat and buckled up. Seventeen now and with his full licence, we were making the most of it.

He pulled up abruptly at the orange on Gillies Ave. David in the front passenger seat turned to me in the back. But before he could speak his mouth fell open and his eyes screamed.

I swung around to see, and my gaze met head on the oncoming truck tearing towards us, out of control, no intention of stopping. And then slam. I was thrown forward like a paper doll into the back of the front seat. We tossed this way and that, as the car became a grinding turmoil of metal, paper, wallets, spectacles, arms and seats hurled through the air, no gravity, in space for an eternity. Then landed in a heap of shattered glass and twisted metal.

A slow hiss of air from the tyres and creaks of strained metal mingled with the eerie silence that filled the air around us. My hands appeared in front of my face. I did a quick check – arms, legs, torso – I was okay. I breathed out. But Josh lay splayed over the dash unconscious as blood poured from his forehead. David moaned, his hand grasping his head. I was the lucky one, unscathed.

Cars pulled up; people hovered helpless not knowing what to do. Concern streamed from their faces. Finally, they wrenched at the doors and hauled the boys out, moaning blood-stained victims their first priority. I stepped out unharmed and unnoticed.

I scrambled about looking for my phone to call an ambulance, but the wail of sirens bore down on us faster than I could find it, a cry of hope.

David sat perched on the curb. His wide-eyed gaze stared at nothing. I enveloped him in my arms, and his warmth filtered through me. Blood trickled down his forehead and into his eyes. He repeated over and over, "No, God . . . No, not Sarah, please, no."

"It's okay, baby, I'm here. We're all going to be fine."

He didn't hear me.

An ambulance officer helped him up and guided him to the

ambulance. Josh was laid out on a stretcher, unconscious.

I leapt in beside them. I had to keep an eye on my boys. The St John's ambulance officers were in full control so I sat quietly trying not to get in their way.

Sirens screamed, red lights flashed as we tore through the wet streets.

"*Hail Mary, full of grace, the Lord is with thee...*" rattled silently in my mind like a favourite song.

"BP 90 over 60. The patient is a young male, stable with agonal respiration showing signs of complete aphasia, suspected subdural hematoma. We need the emergency team to be ready for immediate admittance to the ICU."

The ambulance officer wouldn't meet my eye. It must be bad. I lowered my head and stayed out of the way.

We screamed into the emergency bay – the back doors flew open and a swarm of white-clothed medical staff streamed in and wheeled my men away.

I followed the bustling throng, bedraggled and forgotten in behind. No one came to my aid.

* * *

Hours have gone by and I wait, alone and desperate to know if Josh is okay.

I slip out of the cold plastic chair and glide across the tiled floor making my way easily through the throng of latecomers to the café. I need to find the boys.

The lift doors close; I press the level for the ICU. It doesn't light up. Someone else presses it, the red light fires. No one talks or acknowledges the other. We are all loved ones, waiting and hoping for a miracle. The doors open and there is David down the end of the corridor, talking to the doctor. As I walk up to him, I see his stooped demeanour. The man is patting him on the shoulder, consoling him. Alarms blast through my head as a shard of fear stabs my chest.

I hear the doctor say, "My deepest condolences. If there's anything

I can do, please don't hesitate to ask."

David's resigned nod exudes despair. My panic peaks and my desperate eyes follow him as he slouches into the room. I turn and see our son, propped up in bed – awake.

I rush in and throw myself at him.

"Oh my God, you're alright. You nearly gave me a heart attack, sweetheart." I smother him with hugs and kisses of relief like a kaleidoscope of butterflies in the air. I try to grip his hand but he doesn't respond. He just stares ahead, apathetic.

My husband is standing on the other side of the bed looking bereft, lost. There must be something he's not telling us – something is wrong. I try to get his attention, make eye contact but he's distracted, away somewhere, as if a fog has settled over him that won't lift.

"There's no easy way to tell you this son."

His whisper is barely audible.

"It's Mum – she's gone. She never made it."

My husband stares across the bed through me. My heart freezes as finally I see.

Denise O'Hagan *completed a Master of Creative Writing at AUT (2016). She writes poetry and fiction and has had poems published in a New Zealand Poetry Society anthology, Fresh Ink and a collection from Fast Fibres Poetry Five. She is the author of several novels in contemporary and historical fiction.*

***Johnathan Worrall** is a Creative Technologist (a fancy term for a jack-of-all-trades). When not studying English teaching or veterinary science, he spends his time writing novellas, songs, and poems, illustrating children's books, and making everything from stop-motion puppets to full-sized monster costumes, as seen in the World of Wearable Arts shows of 2016 and 2017. He is currently a film-editing intern for the company Rūrangi.*

A Safe Place to Leave You

Johnathan Worrall

If I were to go,
would you leave your soul behind,
and follow me home?

If I were to die,
would you paint the skies in white,
and lace the trees with snow?

For I've
come to see
the webs on the walls are speaking.

In silver tongues,
they tell me
some wounds are worth keeping.

I know
it's killing me
but I'm lost in my thoughts without them.

I'm alone
but I know
the paint on these walls, it sees me.

And far beyond them,
the valleys grow green and
the trees speak my name.

I
could tell you it's the same;
don't be afraid.

If I were to hold
you and tell you it's alright,
would you believe it's so?

For I've heard you cry –
seen you curse the stars that night
we danced in evening snow.

But I've
come to see
how the lights that gleam in autumn

catch the sand
in your hair –
each strand a fleeting amber.

I'm alone
but I know,
the waves remember us as they will.

And far beyond them,
the wind blows soft and
I've never been gone.

They
say it's all the same.
So don't be afraid.

Too Short to Count Tea Coupons

Madeleine Child

My second home is the Globe but we are mostly out the back in the sheds with our pet collection and the Horse&ShoeSugarCubeClub. We build a rickety aviary and get some homing pigeons and leave them locked in like the book says and then we let them out and watch them fly away, away. Belinda gets bitten by a dead rat the cat brought in and it hangs onto her finger and we have to interrupt Rosalie's speech class. We are in the Duchess of Malfi and have to scream really loud backstage and then be carried on dead. I do Creative Dance with Shona McTavish. I am an ant in something which tours to Tapanui and they drop me off at Raes Junction, and an angel in Hansel and Gretyl but I couldn't twirl around because my costume was all shrivelled at the back where I'd tried to iron it. Sometimes when it is toogoodaday my father takes us to Brighton instead of school and once we took Belinda but Rosalie had already rung in about her having the wrong shoes and the parents all got into trouble. Sally sews herself a rainbow dress for the formal and my father says you're not wearing that. We go to the pool and eat cheese rolls on puddled plastic seats and bounce on the trampolines outside if there's time and leave our wet chlorined towels bundled up till next time. My mother gets lost in the fog up Swampy. Voice of Women ladies deliver great bundles of saved up tea coupons but when we can't be bribed to count them my mother just guesses what they're worth then throws them out. We have Esperanto Club and invalid cookery and make carrots in white sauce in a pie dish. We hang around in the basement at Corso eating the milk biscuits meant for Africa.

Madeleine Child *lives in Dunedin, hoping it will warm up. She has a couple of sons and a dog. She is surprised to find writing is not so very different from making things in clay.*

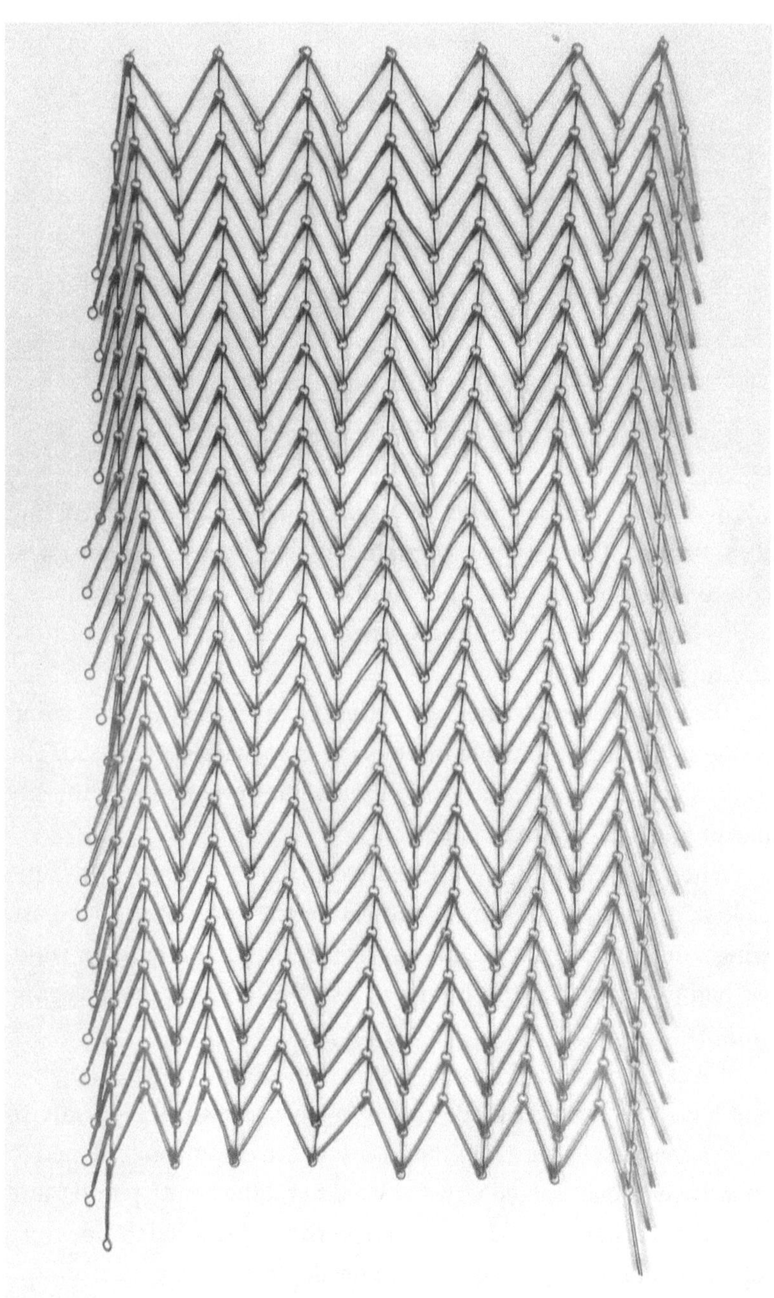

Aramoana — Artwork by Madeleine Child

Still Life

Nataliya Oryshchuk

. . . One autumn day, I became a statue.
This is how it happened.

Angels with broken wings looked down from the crumbling Basilica. The city lay crumpled at their feet. Everything was covered in colourless dust, quiet and eerie. The Basilica angels were lucky. Their relatives from the Cathedral went blind; they got tired and turned to dust.

The whole city was tired, very tired. Many statues lay down and refused to get up. The white marble, the grey marble, the metal. The leaders, the monarchs, the artists. Empty plinths punctuated the city like unfinished exclamation marks.

When the cordons were lifted from the city centre, we came to look at its dust. We slowly and cautiously approached our past, which, until 22 February 2011, was our present. In the autumn wind, we had to accept that the summer was gone, and the city was gone with it.

It was then that I became a statue. I made myself a silver gown and a pair of wings. I made myself a silver crown. I got ready to relieve the tired angels from their duty, because someone still had to watch over the crumbled city. I wanted to fill the empty plinths, and look down at passers-by just like the marble angels used to – because all the other statues were tired, and needed rest.

At first, even passers-by were a rarity. There were no tourists, no families, no couples walking through the city centre. Heavy containers guarded the remains of the buildings, and tall cranes – much, much taller than any statue – looked down at the dusty streets and squares. An occasional builder in a yellow hardhat walked by, preoccupied. Builders did not care for temporary angels. Builders were interested in creating permanent things. The ones that wouldn't crumble.

My angel was too fragile for them to notice. It landed by the broken Arts Centre on the day of a major aftershock. It stepped on its temporary plinth just 12 minutes before the earth shook again. Everything swayed and pulsated, and the earth was angry, so angry. Or maybe it was grieving – but over the loss of what? Humans do not know the answer – but perhaps statues do. The earth kept shaking and shaking until gradually, very gradually, it stopped and rested. But you can never trust the post-earthquake quiet: you never know when the earth will get upset again, and shake all the plinths free of their statues.

The Silver Angel was a child of Christchurch earthquakes. It started its strange, ghostly existence as a spirit of mourning. It wept for the broken wings of all other angels. It wept for their blind eyes, which now saw nothing but the dust. It appeared at the sites of the tired, broken churches and cathedrals. It wept for the earth that shook, and shook, and would not stop. It haunted the city centre, which was now slowly filling with people who came to see the new attraction: a container shopping mall.

The mall itself was a ghost of the old Christchurch. You could almost see the forced smile it wore. The heavy containers came and lined up along one of the oldest Christchurch streets, attempting to cover the ruins; it was slowly soaking up the earthquake dust like a bemused sponge. The containers – now shops – were merrily painted in bright colours. Right next to the broken, forever tired cathedral, they looked like clowns at a funeral.

In the middle of the orange and yellow containers, next to the dead Cathedral, stood the Angel. It was looking at the shoppers, and, quite often, the shoppers were looking back, not entirely sure who or what this winged thing was. "*What* is she?"

People took photos of the Angel ("*What* is she?!"), and the Angel looked down at the passers-by – because this is what statues do. People do not always like living statues; statues are not supposed to be alive. A living statue is a creature of a dream or a nightmare; it exists on the cusp between the animate and inanimate worlds. We humans have an instinctive horror of inanimate things that pretend to be alive; the essence of horror is a child's favourite doll with a sparkle of life in its eyes.

Lifeless that comes to life is the embodiment of the uncanny. Artificial creations are not meant to possess agency of their own. Staring dolls and mannequins provoke terror; humans are instinctively averse to all kinds of inanimate impostors.

Living statues reverse the process: they are humans who pretend to be inhuman. Humans who turn themselves, by their own will, into a *thing*. And thus, they invite trouble. Through separating themselves from other humans, they provoke. And yet, they stay strongly – almost intimately – connected with each and every passerby who reacts to their presence.

I reacted to my first ever living statue many years ago, long before the earth shook, in the middle of the Christchurch Buskers Festival. A new immigrant, I was welcomed by the Gargoyle nestling on its very own gothic plinth by the neo-gothic Arts Centre.

I came to watch it almost every day.

There it sat, a medieval monster in the middle of a busy 21st century street. In a split second, the Gargoyle could transform from an architectural ornament into a living – and highly provoking – creature. It was a *thing* that could come to life in a hundred different ways. There was something childishly innocent and deeply mysterious in this play of stillness and movement. The unexpected interactions felt almost forbidden.

What *is* he? – I kept thinking back then. And many years later, I made myself a silver gown and a pair of wings, and got ready to take the place of tired angels.

It was not easy. I had to let go of the human self-consciousness. Statues do not question their existence. They just *are.*

"*What* is she?" is almost always asked in a loud whisper. It is the most popular question that I, as the Angel, hear. The question highlights the everlasting uncertainty whether a human statue is a "what" or a "who." "What is she?" – demands a small child from her older, and wiser, sibling. The sibling takes a moment to consider. "She is a statue." Another pause for consideration. "Oh, is she like the Statue of Liberty?" That makes the older sibling pause for even longer, then state with conviction: "No. The Statue of Liberty is green!" The younger child is still unsatisfied. Clutching her sister's hand, she takes a tiny step towards me. I look down. "What are you?" – asks the girl, poised for a quick retreat. I let the Angel grin, ever so slightly. The girl grins back, and whispers to her sister, "She is a fairy!"

"*What* is she?" is loaded with a variety of emotions: admiration, suspicion, disbelief, annoyance, marvel, anger. Some people can pass by a living statue without realising that it is, actually, alive. Some people walk as far from the creature as possible, as if in fear of contamination.

Standing on my papier-mâché plinth, I take in everything and everyone around me: the people, the broken city, the lively cafés in shipping containers, the gusts of wind full of fine, post-earthquake dust. I use the wind to slowly raise my arms and let the air fill my long renaissance sleeves. I lift my head and look straight ahead as people pause and stare at me. The angel moved. How can it move? It is a statue. The small crowd is waiting for a while, as if for a miracle. They can't explain what they are waiting for – and why they are waiting for it – but at that moment they experience the uncanny. The statue moved. I relish that moment, soaking up the expectation, unsure of my next move. I wait for something – something in my statue nature, not my human nature – to shift and change. And then, I look down, making direct eye contact with each and every member of the crowd. Slowly, steadily. A child drags a parent towards me.

Another child screams and is carried away by a parent. A group of teenage girls intermittently giggle and scream. I am aware of an older woman, farther away, on the sideline, who has been looking at me for some time, not wanting to mix with the crowd. When all the photos are taken, and the spectators are moving on, she approaches me. She slows down as she passes by without stopping and, very briefly, looks up at me. After a beat, she smiles. I smile back. She solemnly bows her head, as if honouring the human statue on its papier-mâché plinth, and we part.

I chose to haunt the city of the angels with broken wings. I chose to provoke the passers-by through separating myself from them. I am the Other. And when my fragile wings get caught in the gust of fierce Canterbury wind, I open my arms, and pretend to fly.

---

*Originally from Ukraine, **Nataliya Oryshchuk** is a Christchurch-based theatre maker, playwright, educator and founder of NO Productions Theatre Company. With a PhD in Russian Studies, Master of Creative Writing degree and university qualifications in Theatre, English and History, she dreams of building her own theatre guarded by marble lions and gargoyles.*

Daytime Pyjamas

Sally Wilkins

Eva McQueen couldn't remember the last time that she had felt her age. She woke tired. She lay, not quite asleep nor awake, and listened to the morning. The house was a stranger to her, still and quiet. It was Sunday. Her father was supposed to be making pancakes in the kitchen, charred to a deep, smoky brown. Sunday's flavour since memory began. He had tried scrambling eggs only once. It had been a hungry morning. Her mother was supposed to be in the armchair on the porch, legs tucked, the paper across her lap open to the marriages section and Horatio the cat sprawled across her neck. But her father was not in the kitchen and her mother not on the porch. Instead, her parents were dead.

Time passed. She had overstayed her bed. She rose and padded downstairs.

Eyes down, to avoid the gaze of the family photos. Her Aunt Dida had used one for the funeral. They looked happy, in black and white. That's what all the mourners had said. She had wanted to tell them, the mourners, that her mother had left the studio four photos later. The photographer had asked too much of her. She did not cry, she never did, but Eva could tell by the way she curled her fingers inwards that her anger was leaving indents on her palm. Her father, being the man that he was, had bought the most expensive package while mumbling apologies to the photographer.

Somewhere in the attic lay a box of 50 calendars and bookmarks with photos of the three of them. The thought sickened Eva. Her father had intended them as gifts. They were now stark reminders of her new life. "Congratulations, you are an orphan." So instead, she had merely smiled at the mourners. She was a teenager, after all. She was not a mourning person.

A bemused Horatio was perched in a dining chair. Eva was relieved to see him. He had a strong aversion to all human beings except her mother who had treated him as a problematic child and hand-fed him sardines at the table. He had disappeared as soon as the aunts had arrived. Eva had wondered at the time if she had lost him, too. She had a sudden urge to tell Horatio that her mother and, when she thought about it, his too, was dead. "I'm terribly sorry," she began. He hissed at her. It was the first genuine interaction she had had all week.

They had come a week ago, as soon as they heard, and not before a moment's thought. The week had passed slowly. First, her Aunt Dida and her husband Fred. They parked their Corvette on the grass. Dad will be mad, thought Eva. Would be mad. Her parents were grammatically past tense. Aunt Dida and Fred had met in first grade. It was not love at first sight. They had met again at a high school reunion 40 years later, both single and living lives far different from those they had imagined as children. They fell for each other's mutual misery and married five days later. Aunt Dida took Eva in her arms and began to sob. Fred murmured something about getting a casserole into the fridge, eyes looking anywhere but the grief, young and old, in front of him. Aunt Dida was the most maternal of all of the childless aunts. Eva had once confided in her that she would like a cousin. Aunt Dida had left trailing sobs down the driveway. "We all make our own choices," her mother had later said. "Some of them are forced upon us." Her mother never made eye contact when she talked about the past, and so they had sat and watched the dishes drain all afternoon. The subject was never raised again.

Then came Aunt Minou with Hector. Their rental was a hearse. The irony was lost on no one. Aunt Minou had left home with Hector when she was just 16. She had grown up too fast to realize who she was and as a result had a constant air of helplessness about her. She went to her sister first. Hector stood by Eva and addressed the air in between them: "I, too, lost my parents young." Eva turned to look at him in surprise. She hadn't known. Hector was a conversational vagrant. She knew very little about him other than the fact that he lived with a spy novel in one hand and a mound of spearmints in the other. Aunt Minou and Aunt Dida extended their arms to Eva, and she met them as an afterthought.

Aunt Sophie came, as she always did, alone. She parked behind the other two cars, as if to ensure she could make a quick getaway. Aunt Sophie and her mother had raised each other after the two elder sisters had gone away and their mother and father had become more interested in mahjong than being parents. Eva felt shy, looking at Aunt Sophie. They had lost different people, a mother and a sister. They hugged briefly, but it brought no comfort to either of them. Eva became mildly aware of the others in the background, filling the silence with mumblings about the weather and how nice the gardenias were looking and how manicured the lawn and how the traffic on the interstate had been awful. Small talk at loud volume, pulsing like a stenograph word by word until it flatlined into white noise.

Anything said to Eva that day fell on deaf eyes. She stared at moving mouths, until they stopped trying to talk to her at all. She felt as if the tide had gone out of her. The thing that surprised her most about grief was the obligation of it. She felt nothing at all. She knew it would come later, a debt to be repaid with interest. She was acutely aware of her aunts waiting for tears. She couldn't take it – watch a drought long enough and it will be the longing, not the thirst (and yes, they are different things), that will kill you first.

She locked herself in the bathroom and lay still in the empty bath, awash with memories. The faucet curved outwards. Convex, she had learned in science at school. The fact surprised her – it seemed somehow foreign in this new life without parents. When she tired of looking at her bulbous nose from all angles, she grabbed her mother's bath salts, sniffed them and then poured all of them down the drain. Mounds of salt formed around the plughole. She flicked them down with her finger. The act seemed perfectly rational. And so she continued on as she started, pouring the everyday memories of her mother and father down the drain. Toothpaste, shaving cream, face oils, mouthwash, shampoo and conditioner ran down the sink. Her mother had once said to her that one could measure time in cosmetics. Seasons came and went in shampoos, always slightly quicker than conditioner but slower than toothpaste. Years passed in perfume. The empty containers stood up like tombstones around her feet. Eva had stopped the clock.

The next day they had gone to the executor's office. It was hot. Eva noticed that the windows could not open. She was suffocating in a room that could not breathe. Beads of sweat traced contours down her back. She sat between Aunt Sophie and Aunt Minou. Aunt Dida sat in the chair by the desk. They had arranged themselves without thought. Mr Ford, the executor, entered as he spoke–quietly. He was dressed in linen. Breathable, thought Eva. He looked out the window as he mentioned how sorry he was for their loss. Eva thought of her parents lost, collecting dust under the bed like a balled-up sock. It went quickly after that. Her mother and father's words foreign in Mr Ford's voice. To Minou went the dining room table and chairs, the gramophone and record collection, the family china and the entire collection of cast iron pots. To Sophie, the entire library, shelves and all, the houseplants, the family albums, the blankets and sheets and the tiny statue of David brought from Florence. To Dida, the couches, the art, the armchair and the table. To Eva, the house. Eva wondered what on earth her parents had been thinking, to leave her with an empty house. But then she remembered that they had probably not been thinking at all, that they would not have planned to leave this early, that the will would have been written over a glass of wine at the end of a long day like a child's game of mix and match. They had not been willing.

There was no question of guardianship; Eva had turned 18 the previous autumn. This seemed to everyone in the room to be wholly self-explanatory. No one addressed the fact that she did not have a driver's licence, nor that she had never paid a bill. Just as no one seemed to notice as her childhood slipped from the room. The ride home was silent. Aunt Dida's Corvette was not large enough to hold their sadness.

Over the next few days, the house sank into a mood. Everything, that is, except the aunts. The will had turned them into hyenas. They laughed as they scavenged. More than once, she walked in on Aunt Dida measuring the Rococo couches, telling Fred that they must get them valued. Aunt Sophie had moved into the library, stacking books into towers of 'keep,' 'store' and 'throw.' Aunt Minou had taken to playing all of her records. "Listen, Hector," she yelled over the din, "this will do marvellously served with my dauphinoise." Eva could not tell whether Aunt Minou was talking about the record or the blue china serving plate that she was bubble wrapping. At first, the music was a welcome break from empty conversations, though by the end of the first afternoon Eva craved silence. The aunts would break from their plundering for cucumber sandwiches and talk of teenage memories. One would not be mistaken to say that they had forgotten Eva entirely.

It would be rage – the first emotion that Eva would feel after her parent's passing. White hot, settled in the throat just where it makes it hard to talk. She had wandered into the kitchen yesterday, in search of Horatio. A telltale trail of crumbs had made her pause. She followed it with her eyes to an empty biscuit tin. Her mother's shortbread, gone. She knew it was Aunt Dida, that she would have eaten it in one bite. The fact that she would never again eat anything made by her mother's hand unleashed an unrecognizable rage. She did not even particularly like shortbread. But that was beside the point. A child alone should be able to eat their dead mother's food, their one last act of nurture from beyond the grave. She struggled to look at Aunt Dida for the rest of the day, and refused the lasagna she had made everyone for dinner. When she had snuck down into the kitchen for toast later that night, the empty tin of shortbread lay draining, wiped completely clean of all crumbs.

But this morning, the aunts were gone. She breathed in the silence. It was just her, and Horatio. They would return soon, in a rented truck to collect boxes and furniture. Does furniture have a memory? It bears witness to so much of a life, that it almost seems impossible that it couldn't. Her father's armchair bore an uncanny resemblance to him in a way that a dog does their master. She curled up in it. She stayed there for a while, staring at specks of dust suspended in the morning sun, unravelling strands of thread.

A deadline for grief makes the most irrational of thoughts rational. Time was in Eva's hands and Eva in time's. It went both fast and slow and not at all. It made sense in the way that timeless does not mean less time at all, but an abundance of it stretching out to meet the horizon. It occurred to her that she had not said goodbye to her mother and father the morning that they had died. They had left at 8.23 in the morning, her mother's half-drunk tea not yet cold. Eva had remembered looking at the clock and filing the time away, not entirely sure of its importance. For the rest of her life, 8.23 would be her parents talking to her from the grave, a conversation that hung like a phone with no one on the other end. It was suddenly imperative to her that she should say goodbye to all of her mother and father's things. She thought in teenage finalities. She would never see it again, never stay with the aunts again. The thought of being an orphan almost excited her, the ability to stop future conversations dead with both pity and terror.

Without thinking, she picked up the box of records first and carried it outside. She plopped it on the grass. She made eye contact with a black and white man she had never seen but undoubtedly heard before. Then came the books, the china, the rugs, the paintings, the chessboard, chests of drawers and camping gear they had used just once in the back yard. The couches were harder. They resisted her, already answering to a new master. She pushed, socks sliding backwards on wooden floors. Little by little, she emptied the house inside out. A house sounds different with no furniture, time echoes down hollow corridors. She stood in the doorway between the already cooling memory of the house and the harsh light of the new day, between before and after, between then and now. And because there was nothing left to do, she began to laugh, high and clear. A little girl's laugh. She didn't stop, not when she lit the first fire, nor the last. If she had been quiet, just for a second, and listened closely enough, she would have heard exhales of past lives beneath the crackle of the fire.

That's how the aunts found her. Laughing. Aunt Dida got out of the truck first. She let out a strangled cry that got lost in the smoke. Then Aunt Minou, whose pragmatism surprised everyone, as she uncoiled the hose and trained it at the inferno. Aunt Sophie was the only one to met the fire at its rage. "What have you done?" she screamed at Eva. By the time the fire truck arrived, Eva, the fire, and everyone else were dead calm. They stood, arranged like a perfect picture, around a smoldering mess. There was a tang to the air, burned and crisp.

For the first time that morning, Eva realized that she was still in her pyjamas.

Sally Wilkins *began writing a year ago in a small Montreal bookstore in the middle of a snowstorm. She hasn't stopped since.*

Out the Back

Jenny Clay

Jenny Clay *is a writer and researcher. Her poetry has been published in New Zealand and overseas. She's dabbled in short fiction and won the NZSA Graeme Lay Short Story Competition in 2016. She is currently working on a large non-fiction project.*

supplejack pirita
slender black
interlacing   stems
knots
at their nodes
stem tips
spiral
twine
climbing   trees
tie   around
branches
playing   string games
looping
the loop
crossing
and criss-crossing
siblings
tangle
trees fall into
each other's arms
ponga, mamaku
and nikau
caught
by supplejack
skipping ropes
winding
blocking
tripping
supplejack
brings me
to ground   to earth

Artwork by Jessica Thomas

Jessica Thomas *is a freelance illustrator living in Auckland. She is inspired by the natural beauty of the world's flora and fauna. She's currently working on her first children's book, and finding more living things to capture with her pencil.*

Extract from

The Old Man is Shrinking

Peter Graham

Frankie Diamond Comes in From the Cold

The door opened and who should enter but Diamond, Franklin Diamond – you might have heard of him. He's in the dynamite trade. Or carpeting. Brick supplies, home guttering, or something along those lines. He's a big deal in this town, a real swell, a mover and a shaker. I stood up behind my desk as he came in, and we shook hands across it. Neither of us said a thing and he steered clear of my eye, but I caught him looking at my outfit before we sat down. He was a large man, bigger than he looks on television, on his commercials for. . .whatever it was. He had the face of a seagull. His skin was a leather tan. His teeth were over-white, though he barely opened his mouth. Whatever hair he possessed was fluffing out above his ears, leaving the top of his head a bare and liver- spotted moon. He sat with a look of mild irritation, as if there were something wrong with his arse.

Franklin Diamond took a good look around the room, rain falling from his coat. He was all beige trousers and navy blue suit jacket, his coat so wet it was black, whatever colour it started the day as.

"Well, so, what is it I can do for you?" I asked, steepling my fingers, elbows on the desk, playing it nice and easy.

"Huh," he said.

He wiped his face, nodding his head a little, looking up at me. His eyes were blue, light blue, cold blue. And small. His whole face was dry, even with the rest of him wet. We knew each other already; we'd met before in the past and everything about him was familiar, but I also felt like I'd never seen him before.

"I came here because I wonder if you can help me find someone."

"Find who?"

Hands together for a moment, massaging one another, back to looking around the room.

"Gilian."

"Gilian?"

"Yeah, you know – Gilian."

Yes, I knew Gilian. Gilian lives in town somewhere. Lived in town, I think. I mean, I think she still lives here, I think she's still alive, but. . .

"Very good," I said. "And what do you want with Gilian?"

He sighed and kind of heaved around in his seat.

"I don't see how that's any of your business. I need to be in touch with her, that's all. Nothing to do with you."

"Why don't you find her yourself?"

"Isn't that what you're here for?"

The floor creaked outside the door – Dan shifting his weight.

"You can tell me or not, doesn't matter."

Frank nodded, played with his hands, keeping his thoughts to himself.

"Okay then. Let me find her first, before we start telling each other anything," I said.

Sometimes I feel I'm going to be laughed out of the room when I make out my price. Sometimes I am. But in this case, without so much as a comment, he took out his wallet and started counting out bills.

For a short time there was only the soft shuffle of money and the *shhh* of the empty city outside. The overheads glinted off his watch as his hands moved. Nice watch, expensive.

Good shoes too.

He finished counting and handed it over. It felt less than it sounded.

"Dan, out at the desk there will take care of any other paperwork, your details, contact numbers, or whatever. You have any idea of where she got to? Where she worked, last known address?"

"I know as much as you do, kid. We're no longer close."

"You don't say."

Dan and I stood at the window, listening to Franklin Diamond thump down the wooden staircase and slam the door out onto the street.

"What did he want?" Dan asked, holding a croissant.

"Tell you later."

Was it a social call?"

"No such thing. He wants me to do a job for him, that's all."

"What's the job?"

"I'll tell you later."

We saw Frank crossing the square, bent over and hurrying, careful not to slip on the bricks. He turned the corner past the pharmacy and was gone.

"Well," I said, clapping my hands together like a fool. "I'm going out."

I took my raincoat from the hook on the back on the door.

"Well," said Dan after a moment of his own. "I'm going home then." He went out to his desk. "Wait for me."

I flicked off the heater, the radio, the light, the hope, the dreams, and stood waiting by Dan's desk as he spent a good while longer than should be necessary to find the arm of his coat behind him, grunting with displeasure as he realised the arm had been inside out all along.

Eventually we made it out onto the street, wet and illuminated – the street that is – by a buzzing light outside the building door. As for me, I was far from illuminated though certainly about to get wet. It was getting dark. The streetlamps were lit. The rain continued uninterrupted.

"Want to step out for a drink?"

"No, I have to get home tonight. Maree wants me to. . ." he trailed off.

"Ah, Maree. Okay." I shrugged. Dan and Maree – now there's a couple. There's a lot to be said about Dan and Maree.

"I'm going for one anyway."

"Mm hmm."

I fingered the money as we stood in the doorway. It felt dirty; it felt good. I reminded myself to save half of it for Dan but I'd have to avoid putting it through the books so it didn't mess with his benefit. This case was going to be messy enough without getting Work & Income getting involved. I didn't say anything about it – that could wait.

We stepped out and walked north, under shelter for as much as there was to be had. I had a good coat. We walked through the empty city centre, stoic and silent, each bowed into our chests. We parted at the roundabout, Dan putting his hand on my shoulder with a troubled sigh, lending our parting the necessary sincerity and reverence. I slapped his back. He grunted.

"Enjoy your drink," he said.

"Enjoy your Maree."

"Thanks, *hur hur*!"

I skidded a little as I turned away but recovered with grace and headed into the oncoming darkness, down the long road and across the tracks.

Peter Graham *is based in Wellington. His approach to writing is "begin somewhere and find a way", or else, "destruction is as good as it gets." He is working on his first book, a pursuit that seems interminable, but he has hope.*

Morning Commute

Andrew Stiggers

His head throbbing, Phil wakes to the shrill call of a tui outside his window. *That's just great.* He'd had another restless night, worrying about bills and blood tests among other things. And when he finally did sleep, he'd dreamt again about getting lost in the bush. Half-blind in the dark undergrowth, he'd slipped down a bank and found himself circling back and ending up where he started. He'd given up hope.

The alarm clock beeps, and he's off. Loo, wash, dress. Down the stairs and out of the house. There's never time for breakfast.

Phil spies a wood pigeon perched on a tree, its neck nestled in plumped-up feathers. *Smug bugger.*

The road outside his driveway is already busy and he sits behind his wheel, waiting for a break in the traffic. He seizes his chance with a gap before a bus and manages to squeeze into line, but after that doesn't get anywhere fast. The car in front is meandering along while its driver applies her makeup in the rear-view mirror. Furiously, Phil accelerates and overtakes her, the downhill momentum almost propelling him out of control.

What the – some maniac has parked on the clearway and now he's opening his door wide. Swerving onto the median strip and then back into his lane again, Phil feels his heart skip a beat. "For Christ's sake."

He's sick of it all. Phil takes a deep breath. The slog to work through congested streets riddled with roadworks. Late trains and bus strikes. Fighting for a parking space with shoppers out early to scour for Christmas bargains.

"If you're that fed up, find a job away from the city," his wife, Sue, had suggested.

"What's the point? It's the same wherever you end up."

He grips the steering wheel tighter and turns it slightly, feeling an urge to veer onto the lush grass verge.

A school crossing is dead ahead. He remembers their son's Nativity play is later today. He corrects the wheel.

After a period of travelling on autopilot, Phil finds himself going up the highway on-ramp bridge. Beyond the wetlands, the water on the harbour's edge dances in the morning light, the city's tower and volcanic cones prominent on the skyline.

Phil surveys the traffic down below on the motorway. Like the constant ebb and flow of the neighbouring tide, they would all head about their business, and then return home again, day after day. Part of a single, beating, arterial network.

Merging into the slow lane, Phil is surprised by a helmeted Santa on a motorbike riding up alongside him, tinsel strapped around his waist, and laughs when the festive biker speeds away.

With the sun's glow brightening the buildings and trees up on the bordering hillside, he can see far into the distance. He's not lost in the bush, Phil knows. Like everyone else, he's moving forward.

Andrew Stiggers *is an award-winning writer from West Auckland. His short fiction has been published in diverse literary journals and anthologies across the globe. Of Thai-British heritage, he is an immigrant New Zealander.*

Santa's Secret

Katie Furze

It was a typical Christmas Eve at Hana's house.

The evening sun cast a warm glow over the front yard, silvereyes flittered in the feijoa tree, and the velvety notes of Gene Autry's 'Rudolph the Red-Nosed Reindeer' wafted down the hall, through the open door, and out into the air.

Hana and her friend Will sat on the front steps, licking candy canes. Behind them, on the veranda, Hana's dad and Santa Claus leaned against the weatherboards, puffing cigars and sipping a brown liquid in sparkly glasses.

Hana watched Santa chuckling at her dad's joke, his eyes twinkling with merriment.

Then Will leaned in, his hands cupped around his mouth. "Guess what, Hana?" he whispered, with peppermint breath.

"What?"

"My dad is Santa!" Will bit his lip and glanced around nervously.

Hana frowned. That couldn't be true. She squeezed her eyes shut and tried to think. That was impossible. It didn't make sense. Finally, in the grown-up voice she usually saved for her little brother, she said, "Your dad *can't* be Santa – he can't fly all around the world in one night, can he?"

Will shrugged. He didn't seem to have an answer to this, but a splinter of doubt crept into Hana's mind all the same. She pushed it into a quiet corner to deal with later. "Come on, let's play *Justice League*. You can be Superman."

Will agreed, and the two of them left Santa and Hana's dad on the veranda, stampeded through the house, and straight out the back door.

In their game, the villain Two-Face had stolen the biggest diamond in the world, and Superman and Batgirl were hot on his trail. They cornered Two-Face in a dark alley . . . SMACK! POW! . . . and were about to grab the diamond when suddenly Two-Face pulled out a lump of kryptonite. Immediately, Superman's strength started to drain away, he sagged, and collapsed into a heap on the cobblestones. . .

"Ow." Will stared at the beads of blood on his elbow. "I better get a plaster." He headed inside.

Hana followed him as far as the bathroom cabinet where the plasters lived. Then she smelled something sweet and spicy.

In the kitchen, her mum was stirring a big pot on the stove, and her dad, Will's mum and Santa stood nearby holding their sparkly glasses. What Will had said itched in her mind. She wanted to know the truth. She'd ask Santa straight up. He wouldn't mind – kids probably asked him questions like this all the time.

Hana waited patiently for a pause in the conversation, then she took a deep breath, grabbed the arm of Santa's red suit, and before she lost her nerve, she blurted out, "Excuse me, Santa . . . I'm just wondering how you travel all the way around the whole world . . . to every single country, and every single house . . . in one night?"

"Hmmm. . ." Santa pulled on his fluffy beard. "Good question!" He closed his eyes.

Hana waited. For a moment she wondered if he'd fallen asleep, but a few seconds later he opened them again. "Well, the thing is . . . it's hard to understand . . . and I don't tell many people because they'd never believe me. . ."

This was just the sort of thing she'd expected he'd say. Hana leaned in close.

Santa's eyes flicked around the room, then he mouthed the words, "Time travel."

Hana's mouth dropped open. "Time travel!"

"Yes. It's very tiring. That's why my beard is so white, you see." Santa peered at his watch. "Oh my, I need to get started, so you must get to bed. I can't deliver presents until the children are asleep."

Her mum and dad, and Will's mum, all nodded knowingly.

Hana sighed. She had a few more questions but presents were serious business and she wouldn't want to keep Santa from his very important job. She gave him a quick hug, said goodnight, then turned and rushed into the hall.

Will emerged from the bathroom with a fresh plaster on his elbow.

"Santa's going to start delivering presents, so you'd better go home," Hana said.

Will yawned. "We're going anyway."

After Will's family left, Hana laid out a Christmas mince pie and a beer for Santa, and a carrot for the reindeer. Then she pulled on her nighty, brushed her teeth and kissed her parents goodnight.

* * *

A short while later, Hana lay curled up, cosy in bed. The dark blanket of night covered her room. Santa would be coming soon. She listened for noises outside. She couldn't hear any jingling of bells, or any merry laughter – only a cricket chirping. Her eyelids grew heavy. Images flashed in a confusing pattern in her mind – her mum and dad, Will, Santa, her little brother, Finn, the Christmas tree with its flashing lights and the star she'd placed on the top. . .

Hana found herself back in the kitchen, quiet and still, and empty except for herself and Santa. She asked the same question she'd asked earlier: how does he travel all around the world in one night?

Santa reached into his red suit and pulled out a tiny spinning top made of dark metal, like a Monopoly counter. "See this," he said. "This is my time spinner. I go into each home, leave the presents behind, then I spin. In the blink of an eye, I travel back to before I first entered. I do that all night until I've visited every single home, from the Arctic to the Antarctic, and all the places in between."

"Wow!" said Hana. Of course. That was what he meant by time travel. She must remember this.

"I better get moving," said Santa. "Merry Christmas, Hana." He placed the little bronze top on the stainless steel bench and twisted.

Hana watched it twirl, and as she did so, everything around her blurred. . .

Hana stirred in her sleep. She opened her eyes and blinked a few times, then rolled onto her back. It wasn't Christmas day yet; it was still dark. Hadn't she been trying to remember something? Whatever-it-was had sneaked away. Outside a cricket chirped, then she heard a shuffling sound in the corner of her room. Someone was here, fumbling around in the dark. She switched on her bedside lamp and squinted at the brightness. Then she froze.

Someone dressed in a long gown of red velvet stood hunched over her bookcase.

The person turned around slowly. Her face looked delicate, she had white hair tied in a bun on top of her head, and Hana couldn't tell whether she was young or old. She didn't look like a robber, or a baddie, but Hana couldn't remember seeing her face before. She chewed her lip. "Who are you, and what are you doing in my room?"

"Oh dear," the woman whispered. "You're not supposed to see me. I'm sorry. In answer to your question, my name is Nicole, and I'm looking for something special that I lost."

Hana nodded. Nicole didn't seem dangerous, and she knew what it was like to lose something special. She'd misplaced her music box the week before, and she'd thought her life would end without it. "What have you lost?"

"Well, it's only small, but it's very important." Nicole's brown eyes twinkled. "It looks like a little metal spinning top. You probably haven't seen it."

Hana gasped. She remembered watching a small object whirl around in a blur on the stainless steel bench in the kitchen. "Do you mean a time spinner?"

"Yes, how did you know?" Nicole stared into Hana's eyes. "Oh, you know my secret, don't you?"

Hana stared straight back. "No," she said, puzzled. "Maybe I do. . ."

Nicole was wringing her hands. "Hana, there's not much time, and I have a suspicion you can help me."

Nicole seemed so lovely, and Hana wanted to help. She jumped out of bed, took Nicole's hand, and together they ran down the dark hall.

The kitchen lay quiet and still. The black and white checked lino gleamed in the moonlight, and the only sound was the gurgle of the fridge. Hana scanned the stainless steel bench top, but she couldn't see a spinner. "Oh. It was here before. Maybe Santa took it with him."

"Santa?" said Nicole. "Which Santa was this?"

The hairs on Hana's arms prickled. What did Nicole mean? Everyone knew there was only *one* Santa. "You know, the big fat guy with the beard. He visited earlier."

"Oh, I think you mean Kevin." Nicole smirked. "He has his own spinner."

Kevin? She knew that name from somewhere. Wasn't Will's dad's named Kevin? But there was no time for thinking. She must help Nicole find her spinner. "You have to retrace your steps," she said. That's what Mum always told her to do. "Where did you last see it?"

Nicole scratched her head. "In the lounge, I think."

"Follow me." Hana dashed down the hall, following the scent of pine needles.

The Christmas tree looked magical, with its flashing lights and the beautiful star at the top. At its base lay a pile of presents wrapped in festive paper. Hana's heart leapt at the sight of them. Santa must have been already. Her eyes drifted up to the table. Sure enough, the beer bottle was empty, only a few crumbs remained of the Christmas mince pie, and the carrot had disappeared completely.

Hana knelt beside the presents. She spied a big one with her name written on it and was tempted to pick it up and shake it. Nicole cleared her throat, and Hana remembered the time spinner. She sped to the sofa and stuck her fingers down the back of the cushions. "We're always losing things down here."

Out came a 10-cent piece, and a sticky jelly bean. No time spinner.

Nicole smiled, but her eyes didn't twinkle.

Hana peered under the armchair. No time spinner there either.

She lifted the rug, but only a playing card lay underneath. "Do you think someone took it?"

Nicole shook her head. "Unlikely, unless . . . do you have a cat?"

"No. There's only me and my little brother, Finn." Thinking of Finn . . . he always picked up things he shouldn't. Hana had to keep her best stuff out of his reach. Could the spinner be in Finn's room?

Hana raced back down the hall, with Nicole right behind her. Finn's night-light cast a dim glow over everything like a silky scarf. Finn lay in his bed, with all the blankets kicked off, making sniffly sleeping sounds. The cane toy basket in the corner caught Hana's eye.

She crept over and carefully prised out a fire truck, an action figure and a plastic giraffe. If the time spinner was in here it would have sunk straight to the bottom. She glanced at Finn, then gently tipped the basket over, and all the toys spilled out onto the carpet.

Her brother coughed, then turned over.

Hana waited until his breathing grew slow and deep, before she examined the pile of toys. She pushed aside a few rubber balls, vehicles of all sorts, a soft bunny, blocks, a rattle . . . there was no sign of a little metal spinner.

Then, her fingers lingered on a red and yellow wooden toy they'd had forever. She hadn't known what it was before, but now she recognised the shape. It was bigger than Kevin's one, but maybe it would do. She held the red and yellow wooden spinning top out to Nicole.

Nicole looked surprised. "What's this?" She turned it over in her hands and a little smile appeared on her face.

"Will it work?" Hana asked.

"If you believe it will. I think it might."

They tiptoed back to Hana's room. Hana climbed into bed, and Nicole picked up the big black sack she'd left on the floor. Then Nicole placed the red and yellow wooden top on the bedside table, poised to spin.

Hana reached out and touched Nicole's arm. "Wait. . ."

Nicole looked at her.

"Please, tell me the truth. The whole truth," said Hana.

Nicole sighed. "It's a secret, you know. But I guess there's no harm in telling you. Once the spinning starts, we'll go back in time and you won't remember any of this."

Hana nodded.

"The truth is," Nicole began, "the world is vast, and the population has grown. These days there are many millions of children, and Santa's job is far too big for any one person, even with the help of time spinners. That's why there are many of us. It's a huge team effort. On Christmas Eve we visit every single country and every single dwelling – even igloos, huts, hospitals and boats – and we deliver presents to all the children."

"Do you use a sleigh?"

Nicole smiled. "Well, actually, we haven't used reindeer for centuries."

"Do you live at the North Pole?"

"Oh no, I hate the cold." Nicole put her hands on her hips. "Any more questions?"

"No, I guess that's it." Hana sank back onto her pillow. Now she knew everything. And it meant Will was kind of right. She'd have to tell him. Hana pulled the sheet up to her chin. She felt tired, so very, very tired. "Goodnight, Saint Nicole," she said, sleepily.

"Goodnight, Hana dear, and thank you," said Nicole.

As Hana's eyelids closed, she glimpsed the red and yellow

wooden top twirling on her bedside table and the whole room seemed to spin with it. . .

* * *

Hana's eyes flicked open. Light streamed in through the curtains and she could hear the birds announcing the day. She stretched her arms high. What a lovely deep sleep.

Oh, that's right . . . Hana leapt out of bed and sprinted down the hall.

Katie Furze *is a children's author who writes fiction and non-fiction including short stories, articles, plays, picture books, readers, and novels. Her work has appeared in the New Zealand School Journal, The School Magazine in Australia, and in anthologies. Read more about Katie at katiefurze.com*

Fire Escape — Photo by Emma Robinson

***Emma Robinson** is a writer and photographer. Her stories and photos have been previously published in Fresh Ink, Café Reader and Headland. She produces photographic cards as 'emmacards'.*

The Hoarder

Kathryn van Beek

Talia stands gingerly on the caravan step. She wears her polyester blazer and her court shoes on client visits. But perhaps she should wear gumboots. And a hazard suit. As Talia speaks, she sees Pam's eyes narrow in her weathered face. It's hard to gain someone's trust when you're always taking things from them. Their thinly-spun illusions of control. The ability to choose how they spend their Thursday afternoons.

"I'm not going," Pam says.

"Even if you don't go, the taxpayers still have to pay," Talia says. She enunciates her words clearly, hoping they'll parachute over the fence and into the next-door neighbour's garden.

"That's my bloody money!" Ivan shouts from behind the rhododendrons. "I didn't work for 50 bloody years to pay for a no-hoper like you!" Ivan whisks some leaves off for effect. Snip-snip-snip! He always comes out and pretends to be gardening when Talia's here. As though hoping she might shore up his ebbing Kiwi dream.

"Okay," Pam says loudly. "I'll go next time."

Talia smiles. One lives in hope.

"How have you been since I last saw you?"

Pam leans forward so she can share her news without Ivan overhearing. "I got a deal on washing powder," she says conspiratorially. "Thirty kilograms for two dollars. The clothes come out so much cleaner."

Talia nods. Come to think of it, there is a new aroma radiating from the caravan, a chemical twist on the usual smells of rot and ammonia. She doesn't ask Pam how she's washing her clothes. There's a washing machine behind the caravan, but it wouldn't work even if it were connected to a power source.

"Last time I was here you were dealing with some kind of conjunctivitis outbreak," Talia says. "Has that cleared up?"

"Yes." Pam nods.

Talia peers around the entrance to the caravan. Four cats with red-rimmed eyes stare back at her from their newspaper perches.

"I made a saline solution," Pam says. She shuffles backwards, manoeuvring her way between a stack of old electronics and a pile of damp-looking boxes. She produces a jar with liquid in it. Talia can't tell if it's the jar that's green, or the liquid.

"And then I just dab it on with this," Pam says, picking up what looks like a child's sock. She clocks Talia's aghast expression. "It's old, but it's clean. It was Daisy's. It's very hygienic. I think their eyes will come right in a day or two."

"And you're doing this to all the cats?"

"Yes."

"How often?"

Pam runs a hand over her muddy grey curls. "Twice a day?"

"Twice a day. And how many cats do you have at the moment?"

"Seven?"

"She's got at least fifteen of the bloody things!" shouts Ivan from over the fence. "I've been counting!"

Leaving her feet firmly planted on the step, Talia leans a bit further into the caravan. It certainly smells as though there are fifteen cats in here. Something that looks like an old fox fur stole opens its wet red eyes and stares at her.

"You've got a lot on your plate," Talia says. "I brought a couple of cat carriers with me. Can I take two of these guys to the vet?"

"They don't need a vet. They've got me." Pam advances on a cowering feline, sock in hand. The cat hisses and slinks into a dark crevice. Pam straightens and looks around for her next patient.

"You'll still have thirteen that you can keep treating with the salt water," Talia says. "Thirteen's more than enough for a busy lady like you."

"The thing is," says Pam, waggling the sock for emphasis, "these are very special cats. There's a special way to handle them. And the vet won't know how to do it right."

Talia raises a finger in the air as though remembering something. "I've got two big bags of Friskies in my car," she says. "The biggest you can buy. I'll swap you two big bags of cat food for a temporary loan of two cats. And I'll bring them back as soon as they're better."

Talia walks to the battered health board pool car and heaves the sacks of Friskies from the back seat. She grips the colourful handles with her fingers. Her left hand still feels naked without the rings. Funny what you can bear losing, and what you can't. She returns with the sacks and plonks them outside the caravan. Pam's eyes gleam. Talia returns to the car and comes back again, this time with the cat carriers. Pam's interest in the Friskies vaporises.

"No," she says, "Absolutely not."

"It's best for the cats if you let me get them treated. You don't want this place to become a health hazard." Talia says it loudly, hoping Ivan will back her up.

"It already is a bloody hazard," he calls from over the fence. "Let her take the cats or I'll call the council, and they'll make you get rid of the whole bloody lot!"

Pam draws her arms sulkily over her chest.

Talia clears a space in the caravan entrance with her foot, and then upends the yawning carriers. She reaches into her pocket and pulls out a packet of cat treats. "Here, kitty, kitty."

"That's not how you do it. You'll never catch them that way."

But as soon as Talia opens the packet she's surrounded by emaciated cats. It's not hard to grab two from the throng and wrestle them into the cages. The fox fur doesn't stir from its newspaper cave; it just gazes on with dripping eyes. Another cat with a suspiciously large belly stays just out of reach. But she's got two. That's a start. Talia picks up a cage in each hand and trudges back towards the car, the chunky heels of her shoes sinking into the boggy grass. She buckles the cages into the back seat. Pam hovers by the car like a ghost. Talia reaches into her handbag and pulls out a tiny plastic pinball game.

"My son didn't want his Happy Meal toy," she says. "Do you know anyone who might?"

"Oh yes," Pam says, whisking the toy from Talia's hand like a chicken snatching some feed. "Yes, my friend would have a use for that. Just perfect."

"Make sure you go to that appointment, okay?" Talia says. "Not everyone's as lucky as you. You get VIP treatment."

Talia gets in her car and does a U-turn in front of Ivan's bungalow. It's one of the tidiest houses on this little street. As she drives away, she looks in the rear-view mirror and sees Pam hauling the sacks of Friskies into the caravan. That's 90 bucks she's never going to see again. She didn't want to lie to Pam. But there's no way that she, or Pam, can afford the vet. And there's no way her work will cover it. So the cats are going to the SPCA to be put down. Because no one's going to adopt these yowling, red-eyed fleabags. Talia turns the radio up. Perhaps the next time she's got a spare $90 she'll be able to take two more cats. Or perhaps she'll buy a big, bright ring to fill that empty space on her left hand.

* * *

Pam puts the ticket in the side pocket of her shopping trundler with all the other tickets. The bus is okay but it's not as good as her car. She used to have a little Toyota. A little runabout. It got her and the kids from A to B. It was their own private space, filled with all their special things. But then the gearbox went, and she couldn't afford to fix it. The car sat behind the house until it rusted. And when they finally got kicked out, the car stayed. That's when things started going bad. One tiny spot of decay got into her life, and suddenly everything around her was rotting and none of her old tricks worked anymore.

"Did someone ring the bell?" asks the driver.

Pam stands up and steps out onto the pavement, the trundler landing behind her with a thud. It's packed to the brim with things that might come in handy. Always pays to be prepared. A group of laughing tweens passes her, and she does a double-take. Sometimes she thinks she sees Hayden or Daisy on these city streets. But Daisy's in Berlin, and Hayden's in the Catlins. And neither of them are small, blonde or smiling anymore. The city throbs around her. All these town people with all their town things. With all their plastic shopping bags, filled to the brim. Consumers, that's what they are. It's people like Pam who'll save the world. It's the three Rs. Reuse, recycle – well, she prefers to upcycle – and what's the other one? She can check when she gets home. She took ten recycling brochures from the stand at the library in case she lost some. They're in the caravan under the stack of brochures about composting. She's saving her food scraps but she hasn't gotten around to composting them, yet.

Pam walks around the corner and up to the old, stone building. It's cold and imposing, not homely like her caravan, but the thought of Ivan and his flashing secateurs goads her on. He really would call the council on her. He's just that type. She steps into the dark lobby and calls the elevator. The rooms are only two floors up, but with her knees there's no point taking risks. Much safer to move as little as possible. To conserve. People underestimate the value of conserving things, these days. She walks into the waiting room and sits on a chair near a man in a suit. Rich people have problems too, but they can hide them beneath their tailored clothes. She wears her problems on her tatty jumper, her socks with Crocs, her Community Services Card. In the caravan, she's the queen of her own kingdom. Here, she's a charity case. Another man in a nice suit emerges from Sandra's room, and a few moments later Sandra comes out.

"Hello, Pam," she smiles. "Come on in."

Sandra holds the door open for Pam to go in ahead of her. They're probably about the same age, but Sandra is slim and dressed like an art gallery owner. Sandra has an immaculate honey-blonde bob, and smells like the inside of an expensive department store. Pam shuffles in and perches on the edge of the unyielding Chesterfield. All that's in here is the sofa, Sandra's mahogany desk, Sandra's fancy ergonomic stool and a wall-consuming artwork, abstract as a Rorschach. On Sandra's desk is one thin tablet, one thin notepad, a gleaming silver pen and a lonely silver frame. The place is like a TV set. There's really nothing to it. Nothing to burrow into. It gives Pam the creeps.

"Tell me about your week," Sandra says. As she waits for Pam's reply, she shifts the photo frame in her fingers, by turns revealing the photograph to Pam and hiding it again. She doesn't seem to know she's doing it.

"Nice cat," says Pam.

"Thanks." Sandra turns the photo back around so Pam can't see it anymore.

"British Blue?"

Sandra puts her hands in her lap and clasps them together. "So, how have you been?"

Pam thinks about Flossie and Fang. How she gave them up for two sacks of Friskies. If only the car hadn't rusted, she could have bundled them all up, with all their treasured things, and they'd all be together now, living in some secret place.

"I got a great deal on washing powder," she says. "The clothes come out so much cleaner now."

* * *

2.34am. Sandra moves through her Māori Hill townhouse in navy blue silk pyjamas, an eco-cloth in her hands. If she can't sleep, she might as well clean. Every surface is wipeable or washable. Crisp venetian blinds. Glossy hardwood floors. Her recycling sits near the door, ready to be taken out on her way to work. One empty bottle of Méthode Traditionelle, one empty bottle of sparkling water, and the plastic container the cherry tomatoes came in. Everything just so.

2.37am. She can't wait. She takes her slippers off, slides on her Birkenstocks, turns on the outside light and opens the door. She walks down the stairs, creeps around the box hedging and slips the recycling into the appropriate bins. The sense of relief is akin to postcoital glow. Is that thought funny or sad? Or is it just how life turns out? A showreel of images of her younger self in bed with past lovers flickers behind her eyes. She doesn't know who that woman was, or which one of them is lost. Back inside, she puts her slippers back on and washes her hands. She's always been tidy, but she's become fastidious since taking on clients like Pam. Any sign of anything that approximates hoarding is immediately stamped out. Her wardrobe is ruthlessly culled twice a year. She purges the contents of her bathroom cabinets and her pantry once a month. Her cleaner comes once a week. If Pam dies in her caravan, the authorities may as well set the whole place on fire. If anything should happen to Sandra, her home could be on the market within 24 hours. Aside from the furniture, the contents of her house could probably fit inside her Mini Cooper. And even then, half of it would be Marcel's – his three-tier scratching post, his lambswool bed and his expensive toys.

2.46am. Sandra sits at her glass-topped dining table, looking up at the mantelpiece. At Marcel's photo. Marcel's name tag. Marcel's urn. There could not have been a better companion in the world. Better than the most reliable colleague, better than the most thoughtful friend, and certainly better than her faithless, infecund ex. She misses Marcel's fat little face, the thick pile of his fur, the way he kissed her nose with his. She slides her hand under her pyjama top and rakes her nails over the soft skin of her upper arms. Like the fastidiousness, this habit has become worse with age. It started to increase in frequency after the divorce. If her ex was good for one thing, it was anxiety-relieving banging. But that was a long time ago now. These days she doesn't even fuck her vibrator. She'd prefer to sit here and scratch herself. Of all the self-soothing methods she's come across in her practice, this is the most discrete. She's lucky her anxiety manifests this way. Imagine pulling out all your own eyelashes. Or compulsively over-eating. Imagine having to wear your neurosis out in public like that. She digs her fingernails in deeper. Of course, the scratching got worse after Marcel died. But he won't be dead for much longer.

3.00am. She looks at the clock. She looks at her phone. She'll give them some time to get in, turn their computers on, make their coffee. She allows herself one last, deep scratch. Really, what's the harm? Especially in these pyjamas. They don't show the blood.

3.07am. She dials. He picks up the phone while he's still talking to someone. The sounds of his busy San Francisco office are at odds with her silent kitchen.

"Doctor Kaufman?" She can hear her voice bouncing off her well-wiped walls.

"This is he. Hello Sandra."

"I just wanted to check in."

"Well, things are coming along very nicely."

"Yes?"

"Yes, congratulations. We scanned the surrogate yesterday and it looks as though you're getting twins."

"Twins!" She wants to dance on her chair. "What will I call them?"

"How about Marcel Two and Marcel Three?"

"And they'll both be exactly like him?"

"Well, that depends on how their genes are expressed. But our clones are usually almost identical."

Sandra laughs, a breathy exhale. "He wasn't your average British Blue. He really was something special."

"I bet. I'll send you an email with the scan and the invoice. But in the meantime, you might want to think about booking some flights."

He hangs up, and Sandra looks over at Marcel's bed. It's been de-linted, steam cleaned and draped with a soft, new throw blanket. And it won't be empty much longer.

---

*Dunedin-based writer **Kathryn van Beek** has had short stories published in the Sunday Star-Times, takahē, Bonsai, and Headland. She won the Headland Short Story Prize, and she was the 2018 Creative Hub writer in residence.*

Packed My Hopes in an Everest Chest

Maris O'Rourke

I first saw it at my grandmother's small cottage
in the Highlands: a tin chest secreted
under a rough crocheted shawl she claimed
was alpaca, camel and yak hair harvested
from climbs by 'Himself', hasp-held, across
the front – 1953 Mount Everest – etched in blood-red.

I magicked it to fit my hopeful heart-beat,
whispered *Sagarmāthā, sky goddess*, rolled
Chomolungma, goddess mother of mountains
around my tongue choked with men mounting
her body over and over until:
Well, George, we knocked the bastard off.

I threaded red wool through my pigtails, ice-cast
spells to the goddess, beat drums, journeyed
500 miles to hold babies, stalked snow leopards,
hennaed my hair and hands, wove silken dreams,
packed my hopes in an Everest chest. I was ready.

On Kala Patthar, a forest of stone covers the world
before me. I bow to the sky goddess, my white hair
flows in tune with the spumes from her forehead.
I tuck her into my memory box. This is as close
as I go. Closer than the men who die for her.

Down at Gokyo Ri, I join the yak trains – Tibetan
men on the trail – black hair braided with red wool
wound round their heads like crowns. At Tengboche
I spin prayer wheels. Trekking from Namche Bazaar
I get my last glimpse of her: *Sagarmāthā, Mother, I see you.*

Maris O'Rourke *describes herself as a poet and a peregrina, a writer and a walker. Her work has appeared in a wide range of journals, anthologies, and online. She has been well placed in many competitions and also published a family history, a memoir Zigzags and Leapfrogs (David Ling, 2019) and five children's books – one in Te Reo.*

My Magnificent Cloak

Hannah Davison

I stood on the hilltop, as I had been asked. My mother and father draped the cloak around my shoulders and spread it out far behind me. They faced me away from the people, so they could view the finery streaming from my shoulders. Pride swelled.

My parents made that cloak for me. The fabric was coloured deep indigo, decorated with diamonds, embroidered with golden thread. I wore my hair bundled high for I had a fine fur collar. My cloak was more magnificent than the whole night sky.

When I was a girl I found a little green ribbon. It felt cool to the touch, running between finger and thumb. I was so pleased with my treasure I begged my parents for it to be part of my cloak. They had already chosen the design, but they let me use my ribbon to fasten the cloak across my chest.

"Stay on the hilltop," they said, "and the people will admire you."

Clouds covered the sky and thunder rolled around inside them. My parents went away to take shelter. But my cloak would be safe and warm and I stayed where I had been asked.

Then the rains came. And came. Cold water seeped through my cloak. Indigo dye bled from the fabric and stained my skin. The thread was poor and began to rot. My diamonds melted. They were only salt crystals, not gems after all. In their place, many holes gaped.

The golden embroidery was consumed by rust. Flakes fell around my feet.

The holes in my cloak grew. As they grew, the barer I became. The people crept closer to stare at me. The nights felt as cold as stone.

When there was almost nothing left I decided to leave the hilltop. But the people were angry that they had been tricked. They stood on the ends of my cloak, trapping me.

I tried to run, but the ribbon held tightly across my chest. I thought I might choke. The people jeered, wiping their feet on the tatters of fabric and plucking at fraying stitches.

I started to move very slowly. Thread by thread the fabric snapped. I leant forward against the rags of my cloak and waited. I fell free.

The people kept looking at my cloak, stomping it into the mud. They didn't even notice when I slipped away.

My first sunrise was on a beach. I washed in the waves, scrubbing my skin with handfuls of sand. Driftwood lay along the shoreline, clean and smooth from its journey on the water. I built a shelter there.

In the mornings, I walked with the rising sun, finding treasures as I went. Seaweed, shells, flax, feathers. I began to weave a cloak.

Only my fur collar remained, and from it, my new cloak grew. Made of things I'd gathered at the dawn of day. It fit snugly on my shoulders, fixed over my heart, the ends bound together with a little green ribbon.

__Hannah Davison__ is a Scottish-born, New Zealand-grown author of picture books, short stories for young and old, middle grade children's fiction, a freelance writer, journalist and blogger. She can be found at home on their family farm in North Canterbury with her husband, two children and a range of animals. Find her online at hannahedavison.com, on Facebook at Hannah Davison – writer, and Instagram @ hannahedavison.

Winter

Anne Curran

*

I layer
my bed
with blankets . . .
softening
the edge of my loneliness

*

Anne Curran *is a Hamilton poet who loves to write free verse and short verse poems. She remains grateful to all those editors, poets, friends and family who have inspired her work along the way. She began writing poetry when working as a secondary school teacher.*

The Apple of My Eye

Crispin Anderlini

It's a terrible thing to fear your own child. I don't know how it happened, or really what is happening exactly, but something is off about my son. He doesn't look the same anymore; there's something the matter with his eyes.

I don't mean he's ill, or has poor eyesight. But they don't look right and he looks at me strangely with those fearfully blue eyes. Like glacial chips of Antarctic ice, floating alone on a bitter sea.

They tell me it's not uncommon, and the colour will probably settle on a deep, woody brown like mine and my wife's when he's older – the Plunket nurses overseeing his milestones and the GP we visited for advice a few days ago, that is.

I know I sound ridiculous, and some small, hopeful voice keeps telling me I have this whole thing wrong.

"You just need more sleep. It's a lot to manage, taking care of a three-month-old baby by yourself, and you're worn out."

But that gentle little voice inside doesn't get it. It's not normal for a child to stare like that without blinking, without smiling – to just peer endlessly, right into my core.

The other day I was changing his nappy, filled with an oddly sweet-smelling mess I had to clean from his smooth bottom for the third time, and he just lay there silently eyeing me.

"Hey son, how's it going?" I said. "What's up? What d'you want to do today? A story perhaps? I know mum's away and she's the best at reading them, but I can try."

Nothing. Not a cry or a squawk. He barely even moved, except to raise his hand and stretch his index finger at me accusingly.

"What is it? Did I do something wrong?" I asked him nervously.

One eye closed slowly, the lid creeping over the little blue orb. The other held my gaze and jittered ever so slightly. I can't explain it, but a chill came over me and I was suddenly adrift on that lonely sea – freezing to death with nothing but my failings to grab hold of. A tiny smirk seemed to linger on his lips.

"Are you smiling?" I said in the most jovial voice I could muster. "All right, time for a nap."

I put him to sleep without a murmur, and then sat on the floor in the quiet living room amongst the drifting dust motes feeding on the sunlight stretching in. I cried then in a broken way, holding my unshaven face in my hands and rocking.

"What the fuck is going on?" I finally said in a strangled voice. "Where are you Grace? I need you here."

Thinking about it now, I'm ashamed. I haven't cried since I was in my early 20s, when my girlfriend of three years – my longest relationship at that time – came home drunk one night, packed her banged-up green suitcase with the little wheels, and told me she was in love with someone else and was leaving. That time I heaved sobs into my hands for an hour, feeling wretched and torn, and then I was done. I moved on, moved out of the flat we had shared and drowned the heartache with cheap beer and a couple of awkward one-night stands.

I wish I could just have a few a drinks now, maybe call up some friends I haven't spoken to in a while and have a night on the town. Maybe that would settle my mind, and I could lean on them for some answers and reassurance. But no, I need to figure this out. Why did his eyes do that last night? It's not normal.

"Bloody health professionals, what the fuck do they know," I curse loudly, and then pause, listening. He's sleeping in the other room and I can't afford the precious time it might take to settle him again. "They couldn't even get his name right," I mutter. "It's Dayle, with a bloody *y*. Not so hard to get, right?"

Reaching for my lukewarm plunger coffee, my phone burbles

quietly from the couch. It's Grace checking in with me, finally.

"Hi love, how you doing?"

"I'm good. How's Dayle? Are you guys doing okay?"

"I think so. . .I'm worried about him. There's something up with his eyes."

"What do you mean? Is he okay?" There's fear in her voice. It's not what she needs to hear when she's got a big deal to close – money for the family and all.

"He's not sick or anything – there's just something funny going on with his eyes. I mean, they're an odd colour, but there's this jittering. . ." I taper off, not wanting to tell her what happened last night, or about the awful chill I get when he stares at me.

"Are you getting enough sleep? Are you eating properly? You're just tired babe," she says warmly. "I'll be home tomorrow morning, and can take over for a bit. I'm taking a week off so we can all hang out, as a family. You, me and the gherkin." She chuckles a little at the use of his nickname, smiling down the phone. "I miss you guys. . .Hope you miss me too?"

"Yeah, miss you too, love. Can't wait till your home again. It's been too long this time."

"This is the last trip for a while, I promise," Grace says.

"Sure. I've got to go put on the washing now. Call me tonight?"

"I can't tonight. I've got to take the clients out for a meal to get this contract signed. I'll try and call you tomorrow when I get in though."

"Okay, talk then. Love you."

"Love you too, and give our boy a kiss from Mum."

"See you."

I hang up, and immediately feel the now-familiar fear that he will wake up. The thought of facing that bottomless gaze and that eerie jittering again sends me back to the kitchen to refill my now-empty cup of coffee.

Did I imagine it? The way his eyes moved independently of each other? I don't think so. I certainly didn't imagine the freezer-burn sensation when I reached into his bassinet and stroked his cheek and eyelids – my fingers are wrapped in gauze and they ache horribly. Peeling off the bandage, I can clearly see a burn on my index and middle fingers. It looks like they've been seared by an element on our stove, but there's a bluish-grey tinge around the wound.

We, I mean *I*, had sandwiches last night, so it can't have been that. The two-hourly schedule of waking and feeding is doing me in. Why the fuck isn't Grace here? I know we need the money, and I can't work right now because Dayle needs me.

"You're okay. You must have just burned yourself on . . . something. . ." I trail off, thinking of the day and night stretching ahead of me in one continuous stream of feedings and nappy changes. It's only morning nap time, so there's another. . .

I wake on the couch again to the sound of raucous bawling. "Must have fallen asleep," I mutter.

Getting up from the couch, I go to Dayle's bassinet in our room and see that he's still deep asleep. Looking still and quiet – a beautiful little boy in repose. What was the crying I heard then? It sounded like him, exactly like him.

Creeping back out again, I return to the comfort of the couch, shaking a little. I dry swallow one of the large, oval blue pills the doctor gave me before Grace left on her trip, and lie back on the cushions to rest.

"I think you should start taking them again," the doctor had said. "You're not in good shape and we don't want it to happen again. Remember last time. It's not going to be easy looking after Dayle by yourself," she'd said with a professional concern that irritated me.

"It's nothing like the last time," I say out loud, quickly checking myself and then adding a reminder on my phone to take another pill tonight. It could be just a placebo effect, but they calm my nerves.

That time was before Dayle was born and I hadn't been sleeping properly. Cutbacks had left me without a job, but with a nice payout from the generous government department I was working in, so I was preparing things for the big day and trying to keep busy. It was probably the pressure of becoming a father, but I had a bit of a slump. Grace came home one day to find me still in bed and unwilling to get out. I hadn't eaten all day and was a bit mopey, but I was okay.

It happened a few more times, so we visited a Dr Schiller in her cosy little bungalow. Waiting in this stranger's front room, I wanted to flee, to run all the way home and get back into bed. I held on and heard her out in the small and sterile room next door, all the while wondering what the smell was in the house. It finally came to me when she was quietly scratching notes on a large pad of refill, ignoring me with an inscrutable look that also somehow made me feel included. Cherries! Not the real kind, but the sickly, fake maraschino ones.

I felt dizzy when we left, with a script folded neatly and stored in Grace's oversized handbag. Back home again with the pills, I had shaken one loose from the bottle and swallowed it with a quick smile at Grace. She met it with a strained grin, and then waddled to the bathroom to pee.

Stretching out, I had fallen asleep again. This time I didn't wake until morning – in our bed, with Grace leaning into me and snoring gently. The fear I hadn't realised I was carrying around like an ill-fitting suit had suddenly lifted and I felt great. Pills or not, something had shifted inside me. I stopped taking them after a couple of weeks without telling anyone. What was the point when I felt so much better?

There's a noise from the bedroom, and I'm back in the present – a present in which I'm an exhausted new father looking after my little boy, who no doubt needs a bottle and a cuddle. I make my way to his cot and stare down at his little mewling face. So fragile and smooth-featured, like a quail egg bobbing along in a fast-running stream. What will become of him in this rough world we live in?

No time for such thoughts; he's building up to a cry so I better feed him. Scooping him up, his eyes flick open and I drift along with him back to the living room and the bottle I don't remember preparing.

"Good boy, that's better, eh? You had a good sleep."

My hand starts aching again as I hold him, and I switch sides while he fumbles at the bottle and gives me a steely look.

"Sorry boy, but my hand hurts. You hurt papa's hand and I. . ." I feel trapped by his gaze – paralysed. Words won't come; my tongue is frozen and heavy as steel. My heart clatters in my chest as he stares at me. A leery, milk-drunk smile finally stretches across his face, and the words pour out again. ". . .don't know whatishappening areyoudoingthis, butwhy?"

Going back to his milk drinking, I sag into the welcome embrace of the cushions as the feeling passes.

Before long it's burping time, and he belches loudly as I tap gently on his back. Like a wretched drunk, I think, as he spills a little on my already soiled T-shirt. I haven't left the house for two days, so there's no point in changing.

"That's better, eh? How about some tummy-time?"

He seems amenable, so I put him on the floor and watch as he wriggles about while trying to lift his head. Apparently this is good for them, but it looks like a lot of work to me.

Making another coffee in the kitchen, I listen out for signs of distress as I try and clean the kitchen at the same time as setting up the plunger. There are bottles half-full of milk, glasses, plates, and a pot of some viscous brown stuff I can't identify. What was that? I haven't cooked lately, that I remember, and it smells like shit. I rinse it down the sink and scrub off the burnt crust, thinking it could be soup, as a wailing starts up in the living room.

"Coming Dayle. I'm coming now. Fuck's sake! Give me a break here."

Storming back into the living room, I find him on his back, pulling at his own hair and crying in confusion at the assault.

"Hahaahahaahaha! You egg, what are you doing? That's your hand doing the pulling."

A toy from the growing pile stored in a wicker basket distracts him enough to release his hair, and I sit next to him while he grunts at it.

"I'm sorry, I shouldn't swear at you. I'm the idiot."

Before long it's time for another nap, so I put Dayle back in his bassinet, re-bandage my fingers and take another pill. It's late afternoon – close enough to evening, so should be fine. They don't really have much of an effect anyway. And I've set up the absurdly expensive baby monitor to make sure I miss nothing.

I watch some Netflix comedy show on low and then, feeling lonely and missing Grace, I search for porn on my phone. Masturbating quietly in the evening light is awkward and seems wrong while Dayle is sleeping peacefully in the bedroom, so I take up a book with one eye on the monitor instead. Mid-sentence, I see something on the screen from the corner of my eye. It's a person standing over my son. They're reaching into his bassinet and stroking his face with long fingers. I can't breathe as I stare helplessly at the image. Everything around me is suddenly still, frozen in this terrible cold place I'm caught in. The air is frigid and feels violent on my face. My limbs won't respond as the shadowy person lifts Dayle from his bassinet and cradles him.

I hear a noise, a loud wild cry. Is that me screaming?

"Agggggh! GGetttthefuckawayfromhim."

Freed from whatever paralysis kept me on the couch, I trip and scrabble on the ground to get to the door. Making the hall and bursting through into the bedroom, there's no one there. No strange apparition holding my son, and my baby in his bed asleep.

"This isn't happening," I tell myself, breathing raggedly. "You're dreaming. You just got to get your shit together." I can't think straight. I can't have seen that.

Stumbling outside onto the porch, I sit down heavily on the steps. I take another pill from the container in my pocket and force myself to swallow its jagged edges. The simple routine calms me somewhat as I watch a couple wheel their young one up the street – a little girl murmuring to herself under the stroller's awning while her parents share a joke. Their laughter eases through the stern white fence around our place and mixes with the cool night air to slow my panting confusion.

"Just breathe deeply," I say. "It's all good. Not long now. Grace'll be back tomorrow, and we'll be okay." It helps, this breathing technique, so I take another deep breath to release the tension in my shaky limbs. "We're good, just need to get some sleep. I'll tell Grace all about it. . .hehehe. She'll laugh at me for this weirdness. Better go and check on Dayle."

He's in my arms now, still sleeping but restless, so I whistle a high-pitched tune to relax him as I sink onto our bed. It relaxes me too, as I rock him gently in the cool blue glow of the rocket ship nightlight that has switched on in the gloom.

"We've had a long day. Mum will be home soon, and it'll be okay," I whisper to his luminous face. "Maybe we'll go to the park and you can try the baby swing. You'll enjoy that."

We stretch out together, Dayle by my side with my bandaged hand over his back. It's intimate and so quiet – just a father and his son resting together in the gathering dark.

I dream that we're all together in an old wooden rowboat: me, Grace and Dayle floating on a calm Arctic sea, surrounded by other parents humming a tune I recognise, but can't place. They turn towards us as we drift along, and I see that they're covered in delicate ice crystals that chime gently in a breeze that rocks our boats. The rocking becomes a shuddering, and our little ship starts to tip. I grab at my family and shout for them to hold tight.

"Don't let go," I yell as the icy waters cover us. . .

"WHAT HAVE YOU DONE!? WAKE THE FUCK UP, YOU IDIOT!!" Grace has her face pressed up against mine, shouting things I don't understand. "YOU PIECE OF SHIT, WHAT ARE YOU DOING? GET UP!!"

There's desperation in her voice, but I can't see why she's so upset.

"Whatdyoumean? Calm down. What's wrong?"

Lifting my arm, I see his cold blue eyes staring emptily at the ceiling, awash in the brittle morning light.

The Stand — Photograph by Crispin Anderlini

Crispin Anderlini *is a Wellington-based short story writer by night, and paid storyteller for Victoria University of Wellington by day. Having written on-and-off over the years, he now writes with a purpose in the quiet evening hours when his young son and partner sleep peacefully in other rooms. This is his first short story to be published.*

Olga

Helen McNeil

The Coke bottle lands in the delivery tray. It says *Olga* on the label. The name brings visions of a little pink and white girl-child and blonde parents but the liquid inside is still brown. It's not his bottle but Henry retrieves it anyway and twists the red cap. His hand is steady, but there is a persistent tic jumping under his right eye. It's been a long time since he slept. He tips Olga's brown drink back, swallows, paces the five steps to the doorway and the automatic door opens. As he turns back to the Coke machine, the door closes behind him. He tips the bottle again; it's too sweet but he swallows it anyway. Henry twists the red cap back on, watching the long fingers fumble to get the screw top to slip into place. It's his hand. It's the same colour as the Coke in Olga's bottle.

Henry's father used to say he was toffee but that was when he was six or seven and he sat in the front of the car, on the way to school, in his school uniform of dark green. A Mackintosh's Toffee – mint flavoured. When he was a teenager and he surfed the long left-hand break at Raglan through the endless summer, the sun melted him to a dark chocolate. He'd started out as coffee-coloured, been through shades of cold tea, weak and strong, depending on how long he spent in the sun, and now, at 56, he's Coke-coloured. His candy floss hair is showing spirals of white. Edible or drinkable, that's him. Palatably pink and white on the inside.

The sky is lightening outside. It's 5.37 according to his watch, so it must be morning. He looks around for a rubbish bin but there is none. He pushes the half-empty bottle into his jacket pocket. The phone in his shirt pocket vibrates and he flips it open before the ring can cut in. It's Beth.

"Fiona's in the delivery suite," he says. "With Alice. They won't let step-fathers in."

"You're pacing outside? I'm at the airport – be there in 20 minutes. How long?"

"She went in just after five."

"She'll be alright, Henry, she will. Taxi's just leaving. Hope I make it."

It's been 33 minutes since they wheeled Fiona into the delivery suite, crying, groaning, smiling, one arm cradling her huge green-draped belly and her left hand entwined with Alice's. Only Alice, as her partner, was allowed in with her. Fiona had waved at him as she disappeared through the double doors, and Alice had said, *see you soon, all three of us.* He'd gone out into the vestibule to get cell phone coverage and was leaving a message on Beth's phone when the door into the rest of the hospital slid shut. It wouldn't let him in again. The notice on the vestibule wall said: *For the safety of our patients, this door is kept locked between 9pm and 7am.*

Henry had been born in this hospital. When it was brand new – state of the art. And his father had paced, maybe this same floor, maybe when the cork tiles had shone golden, before they'd been dulled by footsteps, measuring the waiting, waiting. Maybe there'd been a clock to watch, up on the wall, with its minute hand jerking in slow motion. Where had his father been taken to hear the news – a side room somewhere? Just him and the doctor. Perhaps his father had one eyelid jumping, as if it had a life of its own. Had it kept twitching, when his father swallowed the news that he had a new baby son, a coffee-coloured healthy boy? Perhaps he would have straightened his spine, clenched his jaw, against the doctor's curiosity, his unspoken questions. Would he have stayed that way, rigid, frozen, when the doctor told him that the emergency caesarian had gone wrong, they could not save mother and baby because there had been no way that state of the art could stop her bleeding? Had his father felt that his patience with his wife, through months of long silences when she had looked straight through him, had just got him the booby prize?

Henry has one picture of her. She's sitting on the decking of their Kenyan home, a large picture hat keeping her pink English skin from burning, and she's saying something to the camera. The date on the back shows it was taken the year he was born, just before the British Army helped them leave Kenya, to escape the savagery, to protect his white, British father from repercussions. When he asked his father about the photograph, the skin under his right eye would twitch then jump, faster, faster – telling the story, the secret story, in Morse code – dash, dot, dash, dash. His father would sit rigid and Henry would hold his breath, watching that eye twitching, wishing he could decipher it. Or that he could read his mother's lips in that photo saying that she was glad to have this little baby growing inside her, telling him he was welcome.

When he was about four years old, he'd decided that he must be coffee-coloured because he was made in Kenya. He almost told his father. But he couldn't. The agitated skin under his father's eye told him he shouldn't.

Henry rubs his eyes. He can see the bulkiness of buildings outside now, the light pushing them into another day. This baby will be pushed into the world today, this morning that is insisting the city wake up will bring him or her out from the dark, to join the rest of the family.

Maybe he should have gone home after he'd delivered Fiona and Alice safely into the care of hospital staff. He could have waited at home, near the phone, out of the way. He could have vacuumed the lounge or cooked dinner. He could have made himself useful. But Fiona had said she wanted him here, right here next to her in the hospital room as she rode the contractions, because he made her laugh and that helped. He'd been on one side of the bed, Alice the other. They groaned with her, breathed with her, and Henry had told her the worst knock knock jokes he could remember.

Knock, knock

Who's there?

The Mau

The Mau who?

The one man went to Mau Mau the meadow but he was shot for stuttering.

When she was wheeled into the delivery suite, she wanted to know he was outside, cheering her on.

He'd taken in Fiona's want of him, stored it deep.

Sometimes it was difficult to be a stepparent, all those years of Fiona's teenagehood when she'd yelled at him that he wasn't her real father. He'd understood, about having someone who isn't your father tell you how to live your life. He'd rebelled against it with his own father, eventually.

But now, Fiona wants him to be here, willing her on.

The outside door swishes open again. The dawn air is cold, and he shivers. His belly has clenched over the foreign Coke. What if something goes wrong? What if she starts to bleed and they can't stop it? What if they have to choose – Fiona or the baby? He increases his pacing; the door to the new morning can hardly keep up with him – swish open, Fiona lives – swish closed, the baby lives. He's mesmerized by its sound.

Behind him, the hospital door opens. It's Beth. He almost falls into the warmth and into her.

"Where did you come from?" he asks.

"The side door. What are you doing out here? Come on, we can wait outside the delivery suite. My God, you're frozen."

Beth pulls at his arm and they go inside the warm womb of the hospital proper. She pulls him up the corridor where Fiona had been pushed, waving at him from her trolley, to double doors with the light showing above them.

"Is this it?" she asks.

"Delivery Suite One," he says. "That's where your girl is."

Beth reaches for his cold hands and rubs at them.

"She's your girl too, Henry."

He chews at his lip. His throat hurts. There's the ghost of his father interfering again. Stop your crying, he's saying. Stiff upper lip, my boy, you're British. One tear escapes anyway and his nose needs blowing. He reaches into his pocket for a handkerchief, past the bottle that belongs to the pink and white Olga.

"You made it," he says, wiping at his nose.

"The plane ran on my prayers."

"And you're going to be a grandma, any time now."

"Gramps and grandma, that's us. Only the father's via a turkey baster. I hope Fiona and Alice tell us who the donor was. I'd like to meet our grandchild's father."

The skin under Henry's eye is twitching again. He wishes he could decipher that code too. When he met Beth, his father was in a rest home, his mind not living at the same address. His words had gone too. Maybe they're back in Kenya, Henry said to Beth, with his regiment: the men the army had had to move out for their own safety. Maybe he was regretting he had opted to stay to ensure the evacuation was completed and that it had cost him his wife. Beth had said, *it's just possible that your mother loved your father – your real father, I mean.* Henry's eye had started twitching.

There's a soft hum about the hospital corridor. He leans against the wall and bathes in it. It's purposeful, expectant, an in-between sound. He's holding his breath – waiting for what?

It's the double door opening and a smiling midwife. She beckons them in. Fiona is propped up on the trolley in the middle of the room, still draped in green. At first, Henry can't see what she's holding in amongst the green sheets, because Fiona looms so large. Henry has an absurd vision of the Virgin Mother with child, held in light, glowing with their own luminescence. Alice, encompassed by this still space, pushes back Fiona's wet hair. There is a moment when another trinity is made and held.

"Congratulations, you two, we have a baby girl," Alice says, "and you have a granddaughter."

"Come and meet her," says Fiona.

Henry waits, letting Beth move in first. He watches her face soften as she bends over the green bundle to kiss her granddaughter.

"Henry," she says. "Don't hang back."

The skin under his eye jerks. He takes the three steps across the room and Fiona pulls the sheet away. The face is tucked into Fiona's big swollen breast; he can see a perfect, miniature ear. The sheet slips back and there is a shoulder and a hand with tiny fingers clenching and unclenching. His hand comes up and stops. Beth holds up the untidy bundle, blood stains still showing on the sheet. He jams his hands back into his jacket pockets but the Olga bottle is in the way. His eyes wander wildly, from Fiona with her face shining, to Beth, whose face is stuck in a beatific smile, to Alice, who is rinsing out a facecloth in the sink. His hands come up and he reaches for his granddaughter.

"Henry," says Fiona. "What do you think we should call her?"

"Olga," he says. "I think you should call her Olga."

He puts one dark finger out to stroke the baby's white-blonde hair.

__Helen McNeil__ completed the Master in Creative Writing at AUT in 2010 and has since published two novels set in New Zealand: A Place to Stand and A Striking Truth. She has won awards for her writing. She currently lives in Earthsong eco-neighbourhood (Auckland, New Zealand) alongside chickens, organic gardens, lots of compost and constant negotiation.

Trisha Hanifin *writes short stories, poetry, flash fiction, creative non-fiction, has completed one novel and begun another. In 2014, she won the University of Auckland's Ingenio magazine's short story competition with her story, Me and Bobby Magee. Her flash fiction has been published in various journals and anthologies, including Turbine, Flash Frontiers, Headland, and Bonsai: Best Small Stories from Aotearoa New Zealand.*

Your Body's a Pupa

Trisha Hanifin

You wake in the night, lines from an old love song looping through your head. There's no time but this time and your mind's restless, your heart falling into the centre of its loneliness. You're wingless, wounded, and you're listening to the darkness beat.

Will it end like this, with nothing explained? Just the weight of these worry beads strung around your neck – your body's a pupa waiting for morning's metamorphosis, waiting for words to work their way through the husk of your skin.

You remember the dream that woke you: there was an island in the middle of a rolling sea, jagged cliffs that must be climbed and on the rising tide whales, like none you've ever seen, thrashing and enraged, and far too close to the rocks. You climb and climb, looking for somewhere to stay, somewhere to rest.

The hour before sunrise sleep beckons. The whales settle and return to the deep. The cliff face opens like a zip and you climb through and on the other side there you both are, not your real selves but the selves you have imagined, your words clear and sharp and ready to be spoken. Nothing will be wasted or forgotten, and sleep, sleep will come.

Acknowledgments

Cloud Ink Press's aim is to publish new and dynamic writing. We hope that Fresh Ink reflects some of the many voices that make up contemporary New Zealand writing. We therefore would like to thank the writers and artists who have contributed to this anthology including Suzanne Day who designed the cover, and Nina Seja for proofing and editing.

The 2019 collection was collated by James George.

Cloud Ink would also like to acknowledge Southside Group Management Ltd for their support in publishing Fresh Ink 2019. Southside Group Management is a property development and investment company based in Auckland.

Southside Group Management Ltd

www.southside.co.nz

Acknowledgments

www.ingramcontent.com/pod-product-compliance
Lightning Source LLC
Chambersburg PA
CBHW032006050726
47590CB00006B/2066

* 9 7 8 0 4 7 3 4 8 9 2 8 1 *